ADVA
GUARANTEED ANALYTICS

"If data is now the currency of business, then data analytics is the new language of business. For those struggling to use the language of analytics as well as those already fluent, Guaranteed Analytics is a powerful must-read that lays out a roadmap for designing and implementing an analytics program to drive dramatically better business performance. Jim has successfully leveraged decades of working with companies, from start-ups to Fortune 500 powerhouses, to lead us all to better data-driven decision-making."

—MARCI ARMSTRONG, PHD, BRIERLY ENDOWED
PROFESSOR OF PRACTICE AND MARKETING,
DIRECTOR OF BRIERLEY INSTITUTE FOR
CUSTOMER ENGAGEMENT, COX SCHOOL OF
BUSINESS, SOUTHERN METHODIST UNIVERSITY

"As an Olympian and entrepreneur, I'm hardwired to find a competitive advantage. The problem is, I camp out in my right brain where creative solutions are my strength—while data analytics are my Kryptonite. Meet Jim Rushton and his book Guaranteed Analytics. Jim simplifies the tools necessary for any businessperson to monetize data for bottom-line results. His insights have made us money!"

—VINCE POSCENTE, OLYMPIAN AND NEW YORK
TIMES BESTSELLING AUTHOR OF THE AGE OF SPEED,
LEARNING TO THRIVE IN A MORE-FASTER-NOW WORLD

"Finding the order inside chaos is Jim's unique skill—honed from long-standing curiosity, matched with many years of exacting work on real-world data challenges. Jim is a master at letting the data tell the story, while at the same time drawing out that story through deep analysis and hypothesis generation. Whether it's retail, telecoms, e-commerce, or tech, Jim's structured approach works. If there's a nugget in there, Jim will find it."

—CARTER FORRINGER, GLOBAL
ACCOUNT DIRECTOR, ECLERX

"This book is a reflection of Jim's best works. I was fortunate to work with Jim and his company Armeta Analytics, and we benefited tremendously from his thought leadership, his company's methodical data analysis, and the foresight generated via data. If you want to learn how to use data to guide you instead of drown you, read this book!"

—HOLLY DUNCAN, BUSINESS LEAD AND
INTERNATIONAL MARKETING, ELTAMD
INC., A COLGATE-PALMOLIVE COMPANY

"It's easy to produce reports from data; it's a much finer science to derive insights from complex and disparate information that solve real business problems. Jim has long been on the forefront of producing real business intelligence through analytics that delivers real and immediate ROI."

—ROBERT D. MOTION, DIRECTOR OF WORKFORCE
PLANNING AND STRATEGY INTELLIGENCE, AND
INFORMATION AND SERVICES, RAYTHEON COMPANY

"Our long-term partnership with Jim Rushton and Armeta Analytics in mining our own data made the seemingly impossible an everyday event. His insight was a critical component in achieving our aggressive year-over-year growth objectives."

—CARL BRACY, CHIEF MARKETING
OFFICER, ESSILOR OF AMERICA

"Jim has invested his professional career in understanding everything about data and how to activate it as an asset for business improvement. While partnering with him in a previous job at a retailer, we were able to bring an amazing amount of value to our merchandising activities by activating the data we already had available to us. It's great to see him sharing his experience and wisdom with us all so we can all appreciate the power of analytics."

—JENNIFER PAINE, SENIOR DIRECTOR OF
TECHNOLOGY, SOUTHWEST AIRLINES

"I have known and worked with Jim for over fifteen years, and his knowledge and experience in the data warehousing/ analytics field is second to none. This book encapsulates that experience and is a must-read for anyone in the business."

—TODD LINTON, SENIOR SOLUTIONS
ENGINEER, SNOWFLAKE COMPUTING

"Jim Rushton has an unmatched depth and breadth of business analytics expertise. More than simply having a knack for identifying opportunity in data, he knows how to provide the structure to help organizations convert those opportunities into earnings."

—LOCKIE ANTONOPOULOS, DIRECTOR
OF VALUE ENGINEERING, SAP ARIBA
DIGITAL TRANSFORMATION OFFICE

"Jim has a great ability to encapsulate the core business problem buried in complex software systems. This ability has served us well in all our past and present consulting engagements with him and his company, and is a key ingredient to identifying emerging analytics strategies in our industry."

—SAM WAGAR, VP OF INFORMATION TECHNOLOGY,
GOLUB CORPORATION/PRICE CHOPPER SUPERMARKETS

"I have had the privilege to work with and witness what Jim Rushton has achieved in so many projects: a practical way to truly make the most of your data! I am so glad to see that he has finally put in writing what so many decision makers are longing for."

—GUILLERMO FIGUEROA, MANAGING PARTNER
ANALYTICS, AN GLOBAL, MÉXICO CITY, MÉXICO

"Jim Rushton brings to life the 'inquiry culture' needed to create a successful analytics-based approach to generating dramatic gains for your company."

—MARY KELLEY, FORMER VP OF CUSTOMER INTELLIGENCE, CHARLES SCHWAB

"Jim and Armeta Analytics are expert at taking raw data and turning it into powerful knowledge that can help drive your business forward. They are that kid in class that you always wanted on your group project, because with them as a part of your team you know you are going to be the best version of yourself."

—JENNIFER CHAPPELLE, NATIONAL ACCOUNT MANAGER, ESSILOR OF AMERICA

"Jim has a clear sense of how data and technology work together to solve business problems and optimize business growth through analytics. In his book Guaranteed Analytics, Jim goes beyond the data and analytics, straight to the heart of how to successfully implement and utilize the gems of information and the opportunities seemingly hidden in your analytics."

—CHERYL MORGAN, FORMER SENIOR MANAGER, DATABASE MARKETING, VERIZON

"Jim is the perfect person to write this much-needed book on true analytic success. He has the unique broad and deep experience working at the most senior management levels to translate their business model visions into viable solutions across the vast array of data and analytic technologies. His approach puts the cart rightfully behind the horse, and management in the driver's seat."

—CHANNING STOWELL, CHIEF DATA SCIENTIST, HOLLAND PARTNER GROUP

"Jim Rushton provides much more than the tools to increase your business—he is a trusted advisor that is genuinely interested in you and your company's success. His technical knowledge and skills drill down to provide solutions while maintaining a continued focus on your company's big picture."

—RUSSELL ALEXANDER, MARKET PRESIDENT, PREMIERBANK TEXAS

"I began working with Jim Rushton over twenty years ago and still do to this day. Over that time period, Jim has been committed to and led his teams in successfully leveraging leading-edge descriptive analytics for making real business impact. He has done so across industries, company sizes, company cultures, and technology environments. Over the twenty years I've known Jim, he has innovated in how to apply descriptive analytics for even more effective business insights and how to deliver those insights quicker, less expensively, and to a broader audience in a more accessible way. I encourage you to avail yourself to Jim's expertise and learnings in his book Guaranteed Analytics."

—BILLY SEWELL, FOUNDER OF BCS CONSORTIUM

GUARANTEED ANALYTICS

JIM RUSHTON

GUARANTEED ANALYTICS

A PRESCRIPTIVE APPROACH TO MONETIZING ALL YOUR DATA

LIONCREST
PUBLISHING

GUARANTEED ANALYTICS
A Prescriptive Approach to Monetizing All Your Data

ISBN   978-1-5445-0549-7 *Hardcover*
       978-1-5445-0548-0 *Paperback*
       978-1-5445-0550-3 *Ebook*

CONTENTS

INTRODUCTION 15

PART 1: BUYING INTO THE ANALYTICS PROCESS
1. UNDERSTANDING THE BASICS OF ANALYTICS 37
2. HOW ANALYTICS CAN DRIVE BUSINESS RESULTS 57
3. MAKING ANALYTICS A STRATEGIC PRIORITY 75

PART 2: LAYING THE GROUNDWORK
4. BUILDING YOUR ANALYTICS FOUNDATION 95
5. ESTABLISHING WHERE YOU ARE 113
6. SETTING GOALS AS VALUES 123
7. ROADMAPPING, PLANNING, AND PRIORITIZATION 135

PART 3: TURNING DATA INTO INFORMATION
8. SOURCING AND STORING YOUR DATA 163
9. TRANSFORMING DATA INTO INFORMATION 181

PART 4: MONETIZING YOUR DATA
10. WHO IS THIS INFORMATION FOR? 197
11. DELIVERING INSIGHTS 211
12. TAKING ACTION 235

CONCLUSION 245
ACKNOWLEDGMENTS 253
ABOUT THE AUTHOR 255

INTRODUCTION

HOW CAN YOU ACHIEVE ANALYTICS SUCCESS?

It's Sunday afternoon. You're the regional store director of a national retailer with over two thousand locations. Do you know how you're going to help your company capitalize on a $20 million revenue opportunity tomorrow?

Janet does.

Janet has just received a text informing her about this revenue opportunity and how it affects the two hundred stores in her region. She clicks through the link embedded in the text to learn more. The first element of the opportunity, offering a way to capitalize on some products in home goods, is a no-brainer. Janet has observed this same upward trend in sales of these products in prior seasons and has heard similar observations from her peers. She clicks the button that says "auto-reorder," and just like that, she's set the wheels in motion for her company to make an additional $6 million.

The remaining $14 million of the $20 million opportunity has to do with women's outerwear. Janet is interested, but she wants some more information to qualify such a big bet. She pulls up her relevant sales data, checks the trend analysis for social media sentiment in this product category, and immediately begins to feel more confident about the opportunity. However, just to be sure she's making the right decision, Janet decides she'd better visit one of the top five stores in her region.

Viewing her territory of stores, Janet sees that the top store for this department is only forty-five minutes away. She clicks "Set up store visit," selects a time, and leaves a message for the store manager, Steve: "Huge women's outerwear opportunity—let's talk tomorrow." After calendars are checked and the computer confirms the time, Janet does a quick virtual walk-through of that store's women's outerwear department (an amalgamation of the most recent photos between vendors, store ops, and store visuals). She also pulls up photos of the nearest competitive store's comparable department to better understand what's working and what's not.

With that out of the way, Janet puts her phone down,

smiles, and settles back in to enjoy the rest of her day off. The entire interaction has taken only ten minutes—and it was so easy and intuitive that she hardly felt like she was working.

Flash forward to Monday morning. It's eight o'clock, and Janet is getting ready for her day. Responding to her phone's drive-time departure reminder, she sees, based on current traffic conditions, she has thirty minutes remaining before she needs to leave the house, prep, and make it to her store visit. After getting breakfast ready for the kids and the kids ready for school, she jumps in the car and heads out while her phone feeds her turn-by-turn directions to the store.

By 9:15 a.m., she's in the parking lot near the delivery area (the store hasn't opened yet). With fifteen planned minutes to spare ahead of her appointment, she pulls out her tablet to do some final prep, during which she updates herself on some key information.

First, she brushes up her knowledge of corporate management's perspective of Steve, the store manager. Steve is a "trending star" at the company. He has an ambitious development plan, a sparkling tenure, and a young and growing family.

Second, she reviews the summary of the company's last

conversation with Steve, which the system tells her was twenty-seven days ago. Because Steve is a rising star, the organization has made it a priority to keep in regular contact with him. According to the notes of the last conversation, Steve shared his priorities at the time, and another manager had signed off on them. She makes sure to make a mental note of them. She also looks at the profile picture of Steve to make sure she remembers exactly who he is.

Finally, she refreshes herself with the store's performances in terms of sales, labor utilization, employee development, and management to see how it's performing relative to other stores within the organization and the region.

All this took less than five minutes.

At 9:30 a.m. sharp, Janet walks into the store (her tablet gave her a temporary code to open the rear door since the store hasn't opened yet), where she finds Steve waiting at the ready for her visit. For further input, Steve has asked the manager of the women's outerwear department, Krista, to join them.

As the trio walks over to women's outerwear, Janet pulls out her phone and holds it up to the shelves and racks using an augmented reality interface with color coding for the different products. The screen lights up in different hues of green, identifying the exact product opportunities in the department. Underperforming products are highlighted as well, this time varying in hues of yellow, while products in red highlight opportunities for an immediate markdown.

Janet asks Steve and Krista if the readouts they're seeing appear accurate to what they've experienced at the store. Steve and Krista agree, although they're both surprised at how much untapped potential some of these products have.

With Janet's algorithm-powered app as their guide, they begin debating which of these product opportunities with the most potential are capturable, and which make sense for them to capitalize on. They even do a quick review of traffic patterns for this store and see an unexpected recent increase in Krista's area. By the end of the discussion, they have chosen to adopt about 85 percent of the app's suggestions. In just forty-five minutes, they have helped the company seize another $12 million in new revenue—making for a total of $18 million in just twenty-four hours total elapsed time and less than three hours of total combined work hours.

In prior years, such an opportunity might have gone completely unnoticed unless one of the company's merchandising analysts had, by chance, just happened to be paying attention to that intersection of events that created the opportunity. Now, these kinds of analytic insights are delivered to regional managers like Janet *every week* for all relevant products. Not only is Janet's company able to identify opportunities quickly and accurately, but they also have the infrastructure in place to capitalize on it.

SEIZE THE OPPORTUNITY, SEIZE THE DAY

So how were Janet and her team able to accomplish such remarkable results in such a short time? Better yet, how did Janet's company identify this $20 million opportunity in her region, and how was she able to act on this opportunity so quickly?

The answer is analytics.

Well before Janet received that first text on Sunday afternoon, her company's analytics team (and systems) was hard at work, collecting data and running it through a set of sophisticated algorithms. When one of those algorithms projected a potential revenue increase based on quickly forming regional sales trends, Janet's company was able to push that information out to regional directors like her, who in turn were able to synthesize that information, combine it with additional insights, and capitalize on the opportunity.

Today, many companies like Janet's are using analytics to uncover previously hidden opportunities, act on them, and create tremendous value for their business. However, while analytics has always been about possibility—imagine what you could do with all that data—for many years that promise was all but forgotten.

Almost as soon as computing technology was introduced to business, analytics began to lose its way. The original vision of computing technology into business was, "Imagine how useful and powerful it would be if all this information were in one place." That was true whether it was invoices, paychecks, customer receipts, work orders, etc. But around the 1970s and 1980s, it became clear that the most obvious place to start was accounting data. Before the days of computers and analytics, accountants would do most of their work by hand, entering their calculations with pencil and eraser on columnar printed paper tablets. So, first it was applied to automate accounting, rendering the old, manual double-ledger entry process obsolete. It was phenomenally successful at reducing costs—so much so that instead of using these computers for analytics to uncover hidden insights, businesses began to use it for cost reductions via automation. From there, it expanded to other areas of business, simplifying and usually replacing peoples' jobs during the so-named "reengineering period" of the 1990s. In just a short time, analytics had gone from Holy Grail vision to the back burner, as executive attention was focused intensely on cutting costs to keep up with what competitors were doing. Business computing technology had become nothing more than a means of cost cutting by eliminating head count and automating rote tasks.

To be clear, technology was *very* good at automation. For instance, consider all the different processes that happen every time you use an ATM. You can go to any ATM in the world and insert your card. Instantaneously it knows who you are, pulling from a database of roughly 300 million names to determine your identity. Then, it would ask you how much you want to withdraw, all while tracking that you have that amount available in your account and also determine how much money you've withdrawn in the last forty-eight hours to make sure you haven't reached your limit. Even if the power went out mid-transaction, you would be protected so that no money would be debited from your account without your actually receiving it. Similarly, of course, the bank doesn't want to dispense the money and not debit your account even in the case of a power outage. All done in seconds. The "handshake" of a standard transaction is mind-boggling, and yet we rarely stop to think about its complexity.

And yet, despite the wealth of data required to make these systems work, they're all transactional; you can't use that data for anything other than what it was designed to do—

automate the transaction. (Remember what the "A" in ATM stands for?) That database accessed by the ATM might be good at determining who you are, but that's all it's good at. If the bank wanted to see a list of all its customers who have used an ATM three or more times in a quarter, have an average daily balance of $3,400, and live within a specific subset of zip codes, for instance, the system wouldn't be able to do it. Why? Because that system was set up to automate the transaction, not provide insights.

During the decades that computers were efficiently automating transactions, consultancies and SIs (systems integrators) developed very efficient methodologies to manage and roll out these projects, and today these methodologies are used within almost every company's IT shop. While these methodologies are good and useful for their intended purpose (to perform transactional automation), they are a hindrance to implementing analytics projects. It would be better to have someone new and green work on your analytics project than a more experienced person who is devoted to a typical transactional system implementation methodology.

In other words, in order to succeed, you have to go about analytics projects differently. This book is going to explain why—and then show you how to implement successfully.

GUARANTEED ANALYTICS SUCCESS

Janet's experience with analytics is far from the norm. In fact, most analytics efforts are fraught with failure, with as many as 80 percent of analytics efforts fizzling out—many before they're even put into motion.[1]

But why? What do companies like FedEx, Google, and Netflix, who regularly make headlines with their analytics programs, know that the rest of us don't? Why do a select few companies thrive with analytics, while so many others fail?

After seeing project after project fail firsthand, I began to ask myself the same question. My career in analytics has taken me from big consulting shops like Accenture and Deloitte Consulting, to big corporations like IBM and Verizon, and then finally to my own boutique analytics company. Over time, I began to notice a few patterns that inevitably caused those failures.

First, companies generally thought of analytics as a tool solution. All they had to do was buy some analytics software—the same way you would buy software for a transactional payroll, timekeeping, or point-of-sale

---

1. Kevin Rands. "4 Reasons Most Companies Fail at Business Intelligence." CIO. September 25, 2017. https://www.cio.com/article/3221430/4-reasons-most-companies-fail-at-business-intelligence.html.

system—and then call it good. It's easy to think analytics might work this way, but the reality is far different.

This brings us to our second point. Analytics may be enabled by tech, but at its core it's a human enterprise. Without establishing the culture and organizational structure necessary for your analytics program to take root, any effort to adopt it will be dead on arrival.

Analytics, in other words, is a necessarily robust and nuanced process, one that requires a great deal of planning up front, sustained effort, and an unwavering emphasis on how the end information user—the knowledge workers within your company—interact with your data. Unfortunately, too many companies don't understand this. Instead, they jump into the process without defining their goals, the scope of their endeavor, their timetable for delivery, and who owns and will change their actions based on the results of this process. Eventually, they realize they're in over their heads, and the program stalls out. Or worse yet, they roll out a new-fangled tool that doesn't drive any real business change. They claim success, but have only increased expense and added no new value. That may look good at first glance, but without capturing new value, that's a negative ROI.

If this is you, then it's time to seek out another way, as this vicious cycle isn't doing anyone any good. Every time an analytics project fails, it's a black eye on the entire discipline, earning it an undeserved reputation for being unproven, unreliable, and unworthy of the effort. This couldn't be further from the truth. Driven and managed properly, analytics can lead to tremendous gains and boost a company's bottom line. An analytics program should be cause for celebration rather than hand-wringing and finger-pointing.

Eager to give analytics a better name and guarantee the success these companies had long been craving, I helped found Armeta Analytics. Since then, we have helped numerous Fortune 1000 companies deploy analytics to look beyond the obvious and monetize their data.

These companies have seen firsthand that when analytics works, it's a win for everybody—the company, the vendors, the suppliers, the employees, and the customer. Anyone can create these kinds of wins for their business. However, to make analytics work within your organization, you will have to learn how to play by a new set of rules. The typical approach used in the automation and deployment of transactional systems just doesn't work.

THE THREE TENETS OF SUCCESSFUL ANALYTICS ADOPTION

Analytics is hard work. If it were easy, everyone would

succeed at it. If you've struggled to get your own analytics programs off the ground, don't feel too bad about it.

By following the prescriptive process for analytics success outlined in this book, you will learn how to design and implement an analytics program that will help you monetize your data and drive business results. Driving this process are the following three tenets.

TENET 1: GO BEYOND THE OBVIOUS

Companies often use data merely to confirm the obvious. Everybody knows their best- and worst-selling products, their highest- and lowest-value clients, or their best- and worst-performing employees. The "stars" and the "dogs" are already understood. However, it's not the information on the fringes, but rather the hidden insights in the middle that truly drive business results.

For example, imagine that you run a car dealership. You know your top sellers in your inventory that you never need to mark down, and you know the duds on your lot that you can't seem to pay people to take off your hands. But what about everything in between? How are all those other cars selling? Which take the least buyer interaction time for dollar of margin? Who's buying them and which will become repeat buyers? Which models tend to drive the profitable service maintenance programs? What opportunities are there, and how can your sales team optimize your approach to capitalize on these opportunities?

The majority of the opportunities in your business aren't obvious. If you're only using data to confirm the obvious, you have an incomplete picture of your business. Analytics allows you to look beyond the obvious, take a deep dive into the facts, and use that information to generate valuable insights for your business.

TENET 2: GOING BY YOUR GUT ALONE ISN'T ENOUGH

Your gut is amazing. In fact, it's essential for making good business decisions. However, (1) gut is never better than truth, and (2) gut isn't scalable, while analytics is. Whenever you're making a decision, you want to have as much information as possible so you can base your decision on the facts. When something isn't knowable and a guess has to be made, then let your gut be the difference maker.

For instance, imagine you're a hotel manager and you're interested in driving up your bookings for the weekend. Instead of going solely by your gut, you take a more systematic approach with what's knowable:

· What promotions have you used in the past that were successful? How incrementally different was each?

- How did you approach price structures to entice guests? What was the comparative lift?
- How did your offerings compare with your competitors'? When did you miss the mark?
- What exact events were held in town that weekend last year, and how did that affect bookings? How do those events line up on the calendar this year?

Your data collection efforts are going to help you answer a lot of these questions, but you'll still have some gaps to fill in on your own. For instance, you can see a certain uptick in the data around events, which implies a positive trend, but that uptick isn't enough for you to know what's going to happen in the future.

That's where your gut comes in. After looking at the data and observing how events such as wine tastings, dog shows, and local conventions have impacted your business, you decide that these events will drive increased proportionate demand in the future. So, you decide to drive your advertising dollars toward opportunities related to those events.

Again, gut is great, but it's the interplay between what's knowable and your gut that matters. The more information at your fingertips (facts), the better insights you can derive (gut), and the more likely whatever decision you and your team make will be the right one. You should never have to guess at information that is *knowable*. Analytics helps you collect and deliver a perfect picture of what's knowable so that the only guesswork becomes the art of the job itself—the value that you and your team add as knowledge workers.

TENET 3: FOCUS ON WHAT MOVES THE NEEDLE

Someone told me once, "Don't worry about things you can't control and things that don't matter. And that's 95 percent of things." For instance, Ebola is a constant health concern in certain parts of Africa. That's true, but unless you're a top medical scientist, you can't do anything about it, so there's no need to worry about it in your personal life. Similarly, the color of the interior of your car may be interesting, but at the end of the day it doesn't matter, so there's no need to worry about that either.

There is plenty of data out there that you can collect, but most of it doesn't matter. To succeed with your analytics efforts, focus only on the data that (1) is actionable and (2) drives real value. If it's not actionable, it doesn't matter. If it doesn't drive value, it isn't worth it.

Traditionally companies have had hordes of employees whose job it was to review the daily sales report. These people spend a considerable amount of time preparing to answer any kind of question that may come their way.

They can rattle off all the numbers on command and report on any significant changes in sales, but most of that knowledge doesn't matter. This may have been useful in a different era, but with an automated analytics process, that work is no longer required. If there is a significant deviation in the numbers, your team will be alerted automatically. Otherwise, instead of reviewing a bunch of numbers that they may or may not act on, they are freed up to focus only on the most important action items.

Don't spend your time memorizing reports for the question that *maybe* could be asked. Instead, focus on moving the needle. For instance, imagine you're a recruiter at a big company. There is a lot of data you could look over that might be relevant to recruiting. However, because you're driven only by what matters, you focus your analytics efforts on the data relating to filling positions faster and at a lower cost. This not only increases the revenue capture of high-value employees, but it also reduces overhead expenses—an actionable, value-driven result.

GETTING STARTED

This is not a book about tool comparisons, data modeling, or architecture. Nor is it a book about the underlying algorithms and statistical models that could be used in your analytics efforts. You don't have to be a tool adopter or a data scientist to read this book (though if you are, you may enjoy this book as well).

Instead, this is a book for business professionals that want to make sure they aren't leaving any money on the table. It's a book about making analytics projects successful, regardless of industry or department.

Whether you already own an analytics effort or you're considering implementing one, this book will teach you how to use analytics to make intelligent, monetizable decisions based on good facts and information that go beyond the obvious and speak to the core of your business.

To guide you through our prescriptive process to guaranteed analytics and better decision-making, I have divided this book into four parts:

- **Part 1: Buying into the Analytics Process.** Before building your analytics program, it's important to understand what analytics is, how it can drive business results, how you can make it a strategic priority within your organization.
- **Part 2: Laying the Groundwork.** With a firm organizational understanding of the value analytics will bring, it's now time to begin designing your analytics program. This includes establishing a governance

model, identifying specific goals and values, and finally roadmapping, planning, and prioritizing.

- **Part 3: Turning Data into Information.** Now that you've established your foundation, it's time to get to work collecting and storing your data and preparing to distribute it as information to relevant parties within the company.
- **Part 4: Monetizing Your Data.** It's not enough to generate useful information if your knowledge workers don't know how to use it. This section shows you how to deliver relevant information to the appropriate knowledge workers in a way that helps them understand the data and empowers them to act.

To guide your way and bring our discussions into the real world, I've included plenty of success stories and even some firsthand accounts from business leaders who have utilized analytics to create dramatic gains for their company. Some of these businesses were on the brink of failure, threatened by a changing industry and unsure how to move forward. Others were growing so fast that they were certain that key information was slipping through the cracks and wanted to create a better process for capturing and acting on that data.

Whatever the case, these companies all understood one crucial fact: analytics is both an art and a science. The better systems and processes you have in place to collect data and turn it into valuable information, the better you will position your knowledge workers to thrive. If you can strike this balance successfully, then you will have done what countless others could not—creating a robust and thriving analytics program that will help you identify and monetize hidden opportunities within your business.

PART 1

BUYING INTO THE ANALYTICS PROCESS

CHAPTER 1

UNDERSTANDING THE BASICS OF ANALYTICS

It's 1898. You're the owner of a general store in a small town somewhere in rural America. You live and breathe your business and know everything about it.

You know all about the plot of land on which your store stands. The site was carefully chosen to maximize location opportunities and guarantee you the ideal square footage for the store—and still have space left over for a warehouse in back where you can store some of your larger items.

Inside, all the shelves are set up and aligned precisely as you wanted, carrying all the goods that you personally selected. Customers often remark that you always seem to know what products to carry, how much, and what season. You always seem to have exactly what they're looking for! Considering the nature of late nineteenth-century supply chains, this is no small feat.

But that's not all you know. You also need staff, which makes you the de facto HR department. It's up to you to know how many hours you can keep the store open, how much staff you need, and whether it's best to pay them by the hour or to pay them on commission.

The financial questions don't end there. Do you extend certain customers credit? If so, who gets this privilege and who doesn't? What's their limit? Does extending credit help your future revenue potential, or is it hurting you? It's your job to think through all of this.

Meanwhile, you're also in charge of the store's marketing. Customer loyalty, special events, sales—that's all your job. You're the one who makes sure every kid who comes into the store with their parents gets a free piece of candy. You've noticed that small touches like this bring families back more frequently and encourage them to buy more.

Finally, there are all the decisions you have to make on the fly. Do you deliver large orders? If so, do you charge for the service or is it complimentary? Do you offer bulk pricing if customers order a certain amount of goods?

Every day, these are the kinds of questions and considerations you have to think through—and because you've been at it for years, you're able to make decisions on the fly with a remarkably high success rate.

You know your town, your customers, and your business so well that the decisions just come to you. If a new product becomes available, you know which of your customers might be interested, how much you should buy, and how much you can make from it. Before someone in town becomes engaged, you already have the materials to help her make a wedding dress (you keep your ear to the rail).

In all these ways, general store owners like you were able to create a remarkable sense of intimacy. But while this depth of knowledge was essential for the local general store, it was far too expensive to scale. As the world changed, local general store owners like yourself became a dying breed.

ECONOMIES OF SCALE

Eventually, the world began to change, and after about World War II, economies of scale dictated that it was no longer a matter of knowing your customers and your business inside and out, but rather a matter of inundating customers with so many options in a single space that they were bound to find a product that would work for them. Enter the era of the "Big Box."

Companies like Sears and Walmart were masters of this approach. Presentation didn't matter. Product quality didn't matter. Sometimes, even taking the time to put products on the shelf didn't matter; cutting open a box and throwing it on a shelf helped control cost and drive prices down. This model was impersonal, but it was also efficient, which is why it largely stayed in place until the 1990s and early 2000s.

Right around this time, some of the more enterprising companies began collecting and analyzing data in an effort to boost their bottom line. These organizations couldn't compete with the Sears and Walmarts of the world head-on, but if they could be *smarter* about their product mix, they could gain a foothold in the market. Along with these early analytics efforts came the rise of the internet, and companies like Amazon were able to seize these new opportunities and grow at an incredible rate.

While these companies are far removed from the old general store model, they were able to recognize a defining trait of the general store approach that was all but lost throughout much of the twentieth century: personalization. Modern customers crave a personalized experience, and they are deeply loyal to the brands that are able to provide it for them.

This realization wasn't exclusive to retail.[2] The quest for personalization soon spread to all branches of organizations and throughout different industries. Personalization soon drove recruiting practices, political campaigns, home and apartment rentals—everything. Today, no matter the organization they're interacting with, and regardless of the nature of that interaction, people expect a personalized experience.

In a little more than a century, the world moved from the intimacy of the general store model to the anonymity of the economies of scale model, and then to the data-driven model, which is focused on information distribution and buyer awareness. Today's customers expect the personalized touch again, and companies are happy to oblige. The goal of the modern organization is to bring back the intimacy of the general store owner to their economically scaled business.

This isn't easy to do. It takes a general store owner *years* to accrue the depth of knowledge and intimacy necessary

---

2. Note: As you move through this book, you will see that the majority of examples used have to do with consumer retail. Analytics can apply to any kind of business, but we have used these consumer retail examples because we've found they're easiest to understand for a broad audience. We wanted to avoid using highly specific examples such as IBOT (inbound, on-time percentage). This is a supply chain-specific term that requires significant education for most readers to understand.

to make personalization work. People like that are simply hard to come by—and expensive to try and reproduce through training and development.

ENTER ANALYTICS

Analytics allows you to maintain the economies of scale introduced in the twentieth century and reintroduce the general store intimacy of the nineteenth century. When set up properly, analytics can help lead to incredible insights that, when acted upon, can lead to tremendous gains for your organization, no matter your industry or standing in the market.

Business leaders have been aware of analytics and its business potential for years, yet many organizations struggle to generate the kinds of insights from their analytics programs that they were expecting. Often, the challenge lies not in the analytics process itself, but in the general lack of understanding of what analytics is, how it works, and how it should be implemented within an organization.

That's why, before we dive into the how-to of designing and implementing an analytics program in your organization, it's essential that we first take some time in part 1 of the book to cover the basics, starting with the most important question of all.

WHAT IS ANALYTICS?

Analytics is a process where you take data and the underlying facts and present that information in the fastest consumptive model possible.

So, what does that mean, exactly? In plain English, analytics converts data to useful information that allows you to derive important insights and take action.

In the old days, if you owned stocks, you'd buy a newspaper to track your stocks' performance. One day, shares in your clothing retailer might be up. Another day, shares in your manufacturing company might be down. Whatever the case, the paper would present this as pure data. It was up to you to know the stock codes and be able to decipher their performance.

Any attempt to make that data more consumable to you, the stock owner, is a form of analytics. Even if the newspaper printed colored arrows—green for up and red for down—next to each stock, you'd be able to determine much more quickly which stocks are up and which stocks are down. With less effort, you were now able to assess the same level of information.

Moving from the newspaper to the world of the internet, analytics can now lead to much more personalized experiences. After all, a newspaper is sold to thousands of people, so it must contain information for as many stocks as possible. You, however, only own stock in six companies. You aren't interested in what's going on in the rest of the market. Through a customizable portfolio, you're now able to select and view only those six companies. Suddenly, you can consume relevant information even more quickly and effectively.

WHAT MAKES ANALYTICS SO EFFECTIVE?

The core question driving all successful analytics efforts is, "How quickly can you get from information to action?" The modern world is awash with data, and there's gold hidden in it, but sifting through that data manually takes time, effort, and money—so much so that it's impossible to manage through labor alone.

Analytics removes that labor barrier and, scaled with technology, sifts through the data for you in an efficient and effective manner. Here's why all that gold hidden in your data is so useful.

BEHAVIOR IS PREDICTABLE

As I'm often known for saying: God gave us free will, but we don't actually use it. In other words, our actions are predictable. If we look at and understand what has happened in the past, then we can predict what is going to happen in the future with surprising accuracy.

This knowledge can be somewhat crushing to our egos. No one likes to feel like their behavior fits neatly into a mathematical model. However, the data doesn't lie. While nothing can make predictions with 100 percent accuracy, analytics has proven to be an incredibly reliable business tool, providing valuable information on what we are likely to do next even when we don't know ourselves.

MATH WORKS

You will always have your top performers and your bottom performers no matter what you do. Analytics can help you find that information easily. But thanks to the power of math, the opportunities for insight don't stop there. After all, your top and bottom performers probably only make up about 10 percent of your products, employees, regions, etc. What about the other 80 or 90 percent of your business? How is *that* performing?

MORE DATA = MORE OPPORTUNITIES

When we first begin the analytics conversation with our clients, we like to get a sense of where they are right now. Someone running a grocery store, for example, might say, "Well, we have our store sales data," and then point to their sales by product, by store, and by day. They know exactly how many twelve-packs of Diet Coke they sold in their Dallas store yesterday and how much revenue they earned from those and other sales, but that's about it.

You can learn so much more from the data in a simple receipt.

```
            WELCOME TO BEST BUY #256
            FARMERS BRANCH, TX 75244
                (972) 239-9980

              Keep your receipt!


4242000163-515320-905727-030967-953554

199701 9331 12/27/19      20:51  00882804

9722453   VQ0801W                    2.85
   VISTAQUEST 8-INCH DIGITAL PHO
     40.00 SALE DISCOUNT
     37.14 MY BEST BUY CERTIFICATE
   ITEM TAX 0.24
9873171   DX-TVM113                  2.13
   DYNEX LARGE LOW PROFILE WALL
     50.00  SALES DISCOUNT
     27.86  MY BEST BUY CERTIFICATE
   ITEM TAX 0.17
9742142   MY BEST BUY               0.00 N
   MY BEST BUY ELITE PLUS
   MEMBER ID 2095660179
                                 _____

                    SUBTOTAL     4.98
               SALES TAX AMOUNT   0.41
                                 ===========
                       TOTAL      5.39

xxxxxxxxxxxx0182        VISA       5.39
JAMES E RUSHTON
APPROVAL 028103

OTHER SAVINGS:     155.00
TOTAL SAVINGS:     155.00

MY BEST BUY CERTIFICATE
XXXXXXXXXXXXXXXXXX0734             65.00

THANKS FOR SHOPPING AT BEST BUY TODAY!
YOUR MY BEST BUY BALANCE AS OF 12/27/19
    0   POINTS: 99
GO to MyBestBuy.com FOR MORE INFO

TO A MY BEST BUY ELITE PLUS MEMBER,
WE ARE PLEASED TO EXTEND YOUR RETURN AND
EXCHANGE PERIOD ON ELIGIBLE PRODUCTS
FOR 60 DAYS FROM PURCHASE DATE.
```

Transaction Information

Checkout Timestamp

Location Stamp

Cashier

Any Receipt Special Messaging

Item Scan Timestamp (e.g., how long did customer spend at the register)

Sales Information

Total "Sales"

Couponed Amount

Other Discounts

"Net" Sales

Items Purchased Together

Returns on This Ticket

Tax by Item

Payment Information

How Much of Sales is via Coupon, Internal Points Programs, Cash, Gift Cards, Credit Card?

How Many Separate Payment Types has Customer Used Over the Last 90 Days?

Percent of Tickets for this Customer including Coupons

Credit Card Approval Number

Item Information

Average Return Rate by Item within 90 Days

Average Return Time (in Days) by Item when Purchased with Coupon vs. Without

Certainly, it can be useful for a grocery store to know what they're selling, when they're selling it, and where they're selling it. However, that's the obvious information that everybody's collecting. To gain a competitive advantage, decision-makers at a grocery store could learn a lot more by asking more focused questions:

- How many of those twelve-packs were purchased using a coupon? (What lift is the promotion providing?)
- How many were purchased two or more at a time? (Is there an opportunity to segment customers by usage?)
- How many were purchased alongside a bag of potato chips? (What other market basket possibilities exist?)
- How many of those twelve-packs were purchased by people who bought the same twelve-packs within the past two weeks? (What growth opportunities exist within customer life-cycle stages?)
- If all stores sold potato chips along with twelve-packs at the same velocity, what incremental sales could we capture? (What product affinity sales are we missing by not dragging them along at the same rate?)

The more granular you get with your data collection, the better you will understand your business. Whether the goal is understanding inventory issues, buying behavior, or even which cashiers are stealing, analytics can help. It all depends on what data you're collecting and how you roll the data up.

This is why it's so important to approach your analytics efforts with a clear set of questions and objectives that you want answered. Otherwise, the data might become so abundant and overwhelming that you find yourself pulled in multiple directions at once, leaving you unsure of which opportunity to tackle first.

For example, imagine that you walk ten people through Grand Central Station in New York and ask them to report back on what they see and what can be improved. Even though every person experienced the exact same thing, each will have a different observation. One person might comment on the station's use of lighting. Another might start scheming on ways to improve the square footage of the retail space. Still another might focus on the different kinds of people congregating at the station, how they group together, and what passenger traffic patterns exist.

As you can see, there's no shortage of both information and insights at Grand Central Station. Depending on who you ask and their area of expertise, everyone is going to report back with different observations and a different set of priorities. There's no way to tackle all of it at once, so now you're left with deciding on your priorities—improving the square footage of the retail spaces, improving the lighting and color, or improving passenger traffic? Who's to know what's best? How do you decide?

The trick is to start with an action-oriented goal in mind. Imagine that you and your team are walking into Grand Central Station again. This time, instead of asking them to report back on what they see and what can be improved, you give them a specific question to answer: How can we handle the maximum amount of foot traffic and lowest possible wait times to get on the trains? Suddenly the whole team is aligned around the same goal. While they each may bring their own unique perspective to the problem, they'll be better equipped to understand which facts matter and which facts are just noise in the channel.

Just as you can take an action-oriented approach to Grand Central Station, you can take an action-oriented approach on a sales receipt. *That's* how you build a successful analytics program—not by collecting as much data as possible, but by starting with a goal and organizing available data in a way that helps you make effective decisions. Without this action-oriented approach, you're just collecting data for the sake of collecting data—which is a surefire way to waste everybody's time.

Once you know the action, you can then determine which group should own the effort. Because analytics is a tech-enabled discipline, many companies make the mistake of assigning the ownership of all analytics efforts to their IT department. This makes sense if your target action is IT related (e.g., network security breaches). But otherwise, any analytics program should be assigned to the person or team who is driving the decision-making. If the action is marketing focused, then the marketing team should own the effort. If it's HR focused, then HR should own the effort. And so on.

THE DIFFERENCE BETWEEN DATA, INFORMATION, AND INSIGHTS

Throughout this book, you're going to hear the following three terms quite a bit: data, information, and insights. They may sound similar and each is related, but each is also distinct from the other, so it's important that we take a moment to break them down.

- **Data:** These are facts. Ones and zeroes. You can never change the facts. For instance, when you go to open a work order, you discover that it's already been open for seven days. No matter what spin you put on it, that's a fact.
- **Information:** The story that data is beginning to tell. For instance, after learning that the work order has been open for seven days, you also discover that two other work orders have been opened in a successive manner for the same account over the past twenty-one days, but for some reason, the work still hasn't been performed.
- **Insights:** The opportunity the information is shining a light on. Things you can take action on. Now

that you know an account has had a work order open for twenty-one days, that successive work orders have been produced in a serial manner, but no work has been done, you can put that information into a broader context and then work to solve the problem.

Let's look at an example to see how this might all play out. Say you work at a public water utility. As the head of infrastructure and operations, you need to make sure that planned capacities are easily handled. Through your monitoring system, you learn that pipe 17 has experienced 265,000 gallons of flow in the last hour. That is a fact, but it also has no useful meaning on its own. However, if we put that data into perspective, we begin to generate information. How does pipe 17's flow compare to the following numbers?

- Yesterday's flow at this hour
- Maximum capacity per hour for pipe 17
- Planned flow for today, last hour
- Flow the prior hour and current rate of flow

Once that information is known, the knowledge worker can begin to generate insights that will drive the appropriate actions and monetize your business.

The following table offers a few more examples of the interplay between data, information, and insight:

DATA	INFORMATION	INSIGHT
Twenty-seven hotel rooms were reserved yesterday at Property X.	Those twenty-seven reservations are 22 percent higher than the average daily volume.	Yesterday's "Weekend Getaway" email campaign is delivering an ROI of 263 percent. Let's expand it to additional markets.
A 65 MB file was downloaded by Employee 4235.	It was downloaded after hours and from an atypical website.	This fits the past patterns of downloads that contained malicious content within links. Send a note to the technology security team to follow up.
Pizza Hut location 219's account is sixty-three days overdue.	The owner of these ten Pizza Hut locations has nine accounts paid in full and only one overdue.	We may have a billing problem. Log the issue with the billing department and have the sales rep call the owner to make sure everything is going okay.
Customer Y returned a $300 dress with receipt and tags within seven days of purchase.	Customer Y has returned 70 percent of the items purchased in the last twelve months. That's ten times the average of 7 percent for returned items.	Given the diminished value of returned merchandise (i.e., extra handling, increased markdowns), despite a 45 percent gross margin on this dress, Customer Y's buying behaviors have resulted in a $765 loss YTD. Stop all promotional activity to Customer Y and update the POS terminal so that sales reps can be aware of potential "wardrobing" with Customer Y during the next store purchase.

APPLYING ANALYTICS TO THE REAL WORLD

Analytics can be used to identify and solve both hidden problems and hidden opportunities. However, for this process to work, your knowledge workers—that is, the boots on the ground in charge of converting your information into action—must have access to that information in a way that is easy to understand and even easier to *actionate* on.[3]

We saw how this process might look with the story of Janet, the regional store manager in the book's introduction. Always at her fingertips, whether through her smartphone, tablet, or laptop, Janet could quickly and easily access whatever information she needed to make important decisions. For instance, she knew which products offered the biggest opportunities, what those opportunities looked like within her region, and how she could connect with her local store managers to seize those opportunities.

A good analytics program can help you see key information and opportunities in your business like Janet saw in hers. For example:

- Geo-fencing could help you drive insights into what your customers are thinking when they come to your store but don't end up buying anything.
- Digital footprint analysis could help you gain insights into customer searches—for instance, the keywords they use to search or items they viewed vs. the products they eventually buy.
- Point-of-sale systems are no longer just automation, but rather could help you obtain insights into whether

---

3. As we use it, *actionating* means changing a behavior by taking advantage of an opportunity.

your employees are managing the cash register properly, or even if they're stealing.

For example, imagine you're a franchisee for a popular fast-food restaurant. Your job is fairly simple. You don't have to take care of marketing, design and store layout, menu development, pricing, supply chain for their food and other products, or even the uniforms. Corporate takes care of all of that for you. Instead your main job comes down to two things: (1) making sure you follow corporate processes correctly, and (2) making sure your employees don't steal.

Analytics empowers you to address the second concern quite easily, providing you with more than enough information to answer the following questions:

- Am I getting the normal kind of transactions across my register that I would expect?
- Are my supply costs level with my outbound sales per day?
- Are my deposits by day similar to what I've seen in prior weeks?
- Am I experiencing more voids on my register than I would expect?

By collecting this data, turning it into information, and then using that information to produce insights, you can quickly and effectively identify any problems, take appropriate actions, and monetize the result—which in the case of reducing employee theft means reduced overhead costs.

SMARTER EXECUTION WINS

Imagine you're a general store owner again, except this time it's 2020, not 1898. Everything is bigger now—more products, more floor space, more employees, and more customers. Despite the larger scale, you still have the same responsibilities. You have to know how your store runs, you have to know how your products are performing, and you have to manage all these different needs while providing a high degree of personalization to your customers.

All of this is on your mind as you're staring at your spreadsheet trying to determine which products to reorder. You know what's selling and what isn't—you've been good about collecting the data—but making decisions item by item using that spreadsheet is still a gargantuan task. You can't help feeling like it might not be the best use of your time.

You'd be right. It's a terrible use of your time—something your competitor figured out a while ago. Instead of moving line by line through a spreadsheet, your competitor has scaled up their analytics efforts, saving themselves considerable time and money in the process. With analytics, they're able to use rules and automation to manage 80 percent of their store's inventory. For the rest, they're able to create exceptions in the system and manage the unpredictable one-offs manually.

Here's the bottom line: better insights and smarter execution wins. If you're still running the intimate general store of the nineteenth century, or even the scaled-up megastore of the twentieth century, then it doesn't matter what business you're in; you're falling behind your competitors.

If you want to win—or even if you want to keep winning— then you have to change. Analytics will help your business to better understand your customers, to better deploy your resources, and to better identify opportunities that could be a difference maker in your business. In the next chapter, we'll explore the many different opportunities that analytics can create for your business.

CHAPTER 2

HOW ANALYTICS CAN DRIVE BUSINESS RESULTS

An energy retailer in Texas had recently transitioned from a regulated monopoly to a privatized service. This meant that, for the first time in its existence, it had competition.

To maintain or improve their standing with their customer base, the company sought to create one-to-one, face-to-face relationships with their most important small and medium commercial accounts. The problem was, they had over two hundred thousand accounts they needed to service, they didn't know who the best customers were among them, and they weren't sure how to scale their efforts so that a sales team could accommodate their needs. Even if a single salesperson could handle two hundred individual accounts, they would need at least a thousand-strong sales team to even have a chance at meeting their goals.

Such an approach was a nonstarter. The costs in overhead and labor alone would be staggering, and there was no guarantee such a heavily burdened staff could even create the results they were looking for—even if they worked overtime to get there. If the energy retailer tried to solve the relationship equation through brute force, they would be spending a ton of money to essentially tread water.

Analytics offered them another way. Once we began working with them, we identified a crucial insight the company had been missing: the company hadn't been distinguishing between *accounts* and *customers*. For instance, one of their customers, a wealthy entrepreneur, owned ten different Pizza Hut franchises. Each franchise was its own account, but they were all managed by a single customer.

We didn't change the data—the energy retailer still had two hundred thousand active accounts just as they had before. However, by looking at the data differently through a process we call *family coding and chaining*, we were able to uncover the real story: the energy retailer may have had two hundred thousand active accounts, but they only had thirty-five thousand families of accounts, or customers.

The insights didn't stop there. Once we were able to chain the accounts into thirty-five thousand customers, we were also able to better identify and rank the energy retailer's highest-value customers. Much to their surprise, the owner of those ten Pizza Hut franchises, unknown to them before, turned out to be one of their highest-value customers. They had always overlooked him because, while none of his ten Pizza Huts had cracked their top 10 percent of accounts individually, when combined into one customer family of accounts, the picture was much different. By looking at their data through a different lens, insights like this began springing up through the woodwork.

Through analytics, the energy retailer was able to narrow their focus from two hundred thousand accounts to thirty-five thousand customers, and then down to one thousand top-tier customers—which represented a lopsided 10 percent of the revenues—who they wanted to build one-to-one relationships with. The benefits to their business cannot be overstated. Instead of needing a theoretical thousand-strong sales force to connect with two hundred thousand accounts, the energy retailer was now able to meet the same goal with a mere twelve salespeople connecting with one thousand customers. As a result, they were able to save over $100 million in labor costs over what was mathematically projected.

The distinction between *account* and *customer* may seem

obvious at first glance, but it had been easy for this energy retailer to miss. While operating under a monopoly, the energy retailer only had to focus on two things: provisioning a service and collecting payment. They weren't used to marketing, sales, and relationship management, so distinguishing between customers and accounts had no value to them. Once deregulation eliminated their monopoly, they were forced to adapt to a new reality where customer-centered services could make the difference between success and failure.

MOVING YOUR BUSINESS FORWARD

Like the energy retailer, many businesses are content to stay put; they refuse to adapt until outside factors force them to. Instead of looking for ways to innovate and gain new insights into their business, they settle for business as usual. They bang their heads against the wall trying to solve challenging problems—like contemplating how to serve two hundred thousand accounts with a massive sales force—when a simpler, more effective solution exists.

Here's the reality: if you're staying put, then you're falling behind.

Before we began working with the energy retailer, they were putting in an incredible amount of extra work, with employees putting in tons of overtime in an endless game of catch-up. They looked at those two hundred thousand accounts and tried to solve whatever issues they had through brute force.

This came at a great cost to the business. Throwing people at the problem without scaling your efforts is no way to run a business. An approach like this makes it impossible to think strategically, focus on the true value of your work, and improve the decision-making process. After we were able to chain up their accounts and family code them to get a better sense of who their actual customers were, we were able to reduce the number of decision-makers they needed to call on by over 80 percent—all while helping them segment their customers into high-value, mid-value, and low-value accounts.

In this chapter, we'll be discussing the many opportunities for monetization that adopting a healthy analytics system can provide. As we move through these examples, remember: monetizing your business isn't always about boosting revenue. After all, as the old cliché goes, sometimes a penny saved is a penny earned.

UNCOVERING HIDDEN OPPORTUNITIES

With math, about half of every data set you measure is going to be below the average—but that's not necessarily a bad thing. To get to a good/bad judgment, first you'll need some more context.

Think about the average academic performance across states. No matter how good or bad your state performs, it is a mathematical fact that half of all states are going to fall in the bottom half of the rankings. This can feel embarrassing, especially if your state has been in the bottom half for twenty years or more, but that doesn't mean your state is doing poorly. In any given ranked sample, half of anything will be the bottom.

Let's apply this lesson to business. Imagine that you're selling men's accessories. Your margin contribution reports tell you what's delivering above average and below average.

Margin Contribution By Category YTD ($000s)

	Name	TY	LY	% Chg
67	Men's Pants	$3,499	$3,577	-2%
70	Men's Suits	$275	$299	-8%
71	Men's Sportcoats	$430	$428	0%
72	Men's Outerwear	$2,308	$2,231	**3%**
73	Men's Trinkets	$252	$240	**5%**
74	Men's Underwear	$1,455	$1,533	-5%
75	Men's Suit Separates	$1,637	$1,575	**4%**
76	Men's Neckwear	$1,464	$1,515	-3%
77	Men's Dress Shirts	$2,239	$2,188	**2%**
164	Men's Big And Tall	$50	$56	-10%
172	Men's Slacks	$117	$108	**8%**
173	Men's Belts	$803	$781	**3%**
174	Men's Wallets	$399	$405	-2%
175	Men's Gifts	$1,009	$1,000	**1%**
176	Men's Cold Weather	$822	$852	-4%
177	Men's Sleepwear	$990	$1,033	-4%
178	Men's Socks	$950	$1,007	-6%
500	**Men's Accessories**	**$18,698**	**$18,829**	-1%

Bold ("good") denotes above the average (-1%).

Italics ("bad") denotes below the average.

Margin Contribution By Category YTD ($000s)

	Name	TY	LY	% Chg
67	Men's Pants	$3,499	$3,577	-2%
70	Men's Suits	$275	$299	-8%
71	Men's Sportcoats	$430	$428	0%
72	Men's Outerwear	$2,308	$2,231	3%
73	Men's Trinkets	$252	$240	5%
74	Men's Underwear	$1,455	$1,533	-5%
75	Men's Suit Separates	$1,637	$1,575	4%
76	Men's Neckwear	$1,464	$1,515	-3%
77	Men's Dress Shirts	$2,239	$2,188	2%
164	Men's Big And Tall	$50	$56	-10%
172	Men's Slacks	$117	$108	8%
173	Men's Belts	$803	$781	3%
174	Men's Wallets	$399	$405	-2%
175	Men's Gifts	$1,009	$1,000	1%
176	Men's Cold Weather	$822	$852	-4%
177	Men's Sleepwear	$990	$1,033	-4%
178	Men's Socks	$950	$1,007	-6%
500	**Men's Accessories**	**$18,698**	**$18,829**	**-1%**

But remember in math, one should always expect about half to be above average and half below. And you wouldn't want to get rid of the perceived "bad" here as the *italicized* drives 53% of the total margin, i.e., profits.

$9,904 (53%) of the $18,698 in total margin delivered by the 9 categories performing *below average*.

It's easy to look at this information and say, "These products are contributing below average, and that's bad. We should get rid of them."

Not so fast.

Yes, it's true that half of all your product categories are performing below average (because we just defined what's average based on that data set). But it's also true that, taken in total, those below-average categories account for 53 percent of your profit. If you got rid of all the "bad" products, in other words, you wouldn't be helping your business: you'd be hindering it!

So many of us train ourselves to think that the bottom half of any ranked sample is bad when that's often not the case. After all, half of all Navy SEALS, despite every single one of them performing at an elite level, rank in the bottom half of their group. It's just how math works.

This is where the science and the art of analytics collide. Math works, but context is everything. Without it, a product manager might be tempted to look at that report showing the top and bottom margin contributors, cut out half of their products, and then be left scratching their head three months later when their profits drop off a cliff.

NO MORE GAMING THE SYSTEM

A large telecommunications company (we'll call them Telco) was taking too long to install their products, and as a result, their customer satisfaction numbers were plummeting. To counteract this issue, they implemented a rule that tracked all installation orders that remained open longer than seven days, which they had determined was about the limit of their customers' patience. Soon, the number of open installation orders extending beyond seven days dropped almost to zero.

Problem solved, right?

Not exactly. Despite the new measures Telco had put in, customer satisfaction only continued to drop.

The problem was that Telco wasn't looking at the whole

picture. They were only looking at the fact of the open installation order and whether it had extended beyond seven days. Upon closer inspection, we discovered that employees had been gaming the system in order to satisfy the seven-day metric;[4] as soon as an installation order approached the threshold, employees would close that order and open a new one. Installation orders still weren't being fulfilled within the company's promised seven-day window, but that fact was being obscured through employee gamesmanship.

Analytics discovered something different; we were able to create new insight based not on when the order was opened, but by combining and transforming installation orders by address, we could see when the customer first requested an install. That way, employees could no longer game the system by creating artificial installation orders that masked how long the customer had truly been waiting.

Once we put this new measure in place, customer satisfaction returned back to its original levels.

Without analytics, this problem may have persisted for much longer—and, in fact, it would have even grown worse. The open installation orders would keep piling

---

4.   This will always happen. When management only uses a single metric to track a given goal, that metric will be gamed.

up, customer satisfaction would keep dropping, and the decision-makers would have no idea how to solve it because they wouldn't have the necessary insight. By fixing the issue, we were able to recapture and bring customer service levels back to what they had anticipated. This not only reduced customer churn but also improved labor inefficiencies, since they no longer had people reworking the installation orders.

IDENTIFYING HIDDEN OPPORTUNITIES

You want to put your dollars where you get the most marketing bang. The people at an online dating service thought they were doing this, but for some reason, their marketing efforts weren't producing the same results for their West Coast campaigns, as they were everywhere else in the country.

Seeing this, their impulse was to allocate dollars away from the West Coast and toward other regions better tied to profit. However, something about these numbers felt off.

Analytics proved their hunch correct; their numbers *were* off. As it turned out, the online dating service's marketing team had been measuring the success of their ads based on the day they went out. Headquarters was located in the central time zone, but they would drop their ads by market at 9:30 p.m. local time, when the best prospects would be online. However, a day ends at midnight, and midnight central time is only ten o'clock Pacific time.

Inadvertently, the dating service's team hadn't accounted for the difference in time zones, and this in turn had distorted their data. It wasn't that people on the West Coast weren't interested in this particular dating service; it was that the data only told a part of the picture—only the first thirty minutes of West Coast responses were being included, versus a full two-plus-hour window in every other region.

After we worked with them to identify this problem, the online dating service team was able to measure their marketing campaigns differently, build a more accurate viewpoint of their markets, and allocate their dollars accordingly. Instead of pulling their marketing dollars *away* from West Coast campaigns, they ended up putting more money *in*. Despite their initial interpretation of the data, the online dating service discovered that the West Coast was actually one of their top performers.

In this example, the online dating service was able to monetize their efforts by focusing on an accurate allocation of marketing dollars. The core problem wasn't a big deal—a simple error in measuring across time zones—but it had a substantial real-time impact on the marketing efforts.

Catching this error didn't require an especially sophisticated analytics program. It just required the right people on the job, people who could troubleshoot the subtle problems that arose when a national brand posted content in different time zones. Asking questions like, "When do you time stamp, and how do you define a day?" may not be obvious to most people at first, but identifying and recognizing nuances like these are essential to the success of any analytics program.

COST AVOIDANCE

Imagine you run a department store with hundreds of locations. You have a new line of women's shoes you'd like to introduce, but you're unsure of how to allocate them to each store. Do you go by the average square footage of the store? The total sales of the store? A fixed number to each store?

One chain we worked with, facing a similar problem, wanted to localize, or *micro-merchandise,* their offerings. They were inspired to localize their offerings after watching Macy's have success with the MyMacy's program, which had found ways to specialize their product offerings in different regions across the country.

This chain wanted to do something similar, but in assessing the labor cost, they determined they would need to deploy at least two hundred people to their stores in order to first identify localized opportunities and then execute. However, after they brought us in, we were able to take the data, roll it up in a useful way, create guardrails, and even provide an infrastructure for simple image capture of specific items in a way that helped them identify and manage sales opportunities in specific locations.

Most importantly, we determined that this could all be done with just eight people—well below the two hundred people the leadership team thought they would need.

Here, the monetization opportunity came through both improved sales and cost avoidance. An analytics-based approach saved this company the considerable (theoretical, as they would never have taken that on) expense of deploying two hundred total people to their stores when we determined they could get the same results with just eight.

BETTER HIRING AND RELATIONSHIP MANAGEMENT

Not all monetizing opportunities are on the sales end. Even in the world of human resources (HR), analytics can be deployed to improve efficiency in your relationship and candidate management practices.

In many companies, the hiring process goes something

like this. One business unit or another notifies HR that they need a certain position filled. HR then puts out ads and hires headhunters so that they can gather as many candidates as possible. Once the candidate pool is sufficiently large, they begin the interviewing and vetting process.

For argument's sake, let's say that on average, twenty-two candidates emerge over a ten-week period during every recruiting round. Of those, six candidates may be highly qualified, but the company is only able to make an offer to one of them. Afterward, most companies would lose track of those other five runners-up. They may say that they'll keep those candidates' resumes on file, but in practice, that's rarely the case. Then, the next time they're hiring for the same or similar position, HR starts their search all over again from scratch.

That's inefficient. If a company liked five other candidates almost as much as the person it ultimately hired, why not stay in contact with those five candidates and then quickly throw them back into the hiring mix the next time around? Doing so would save both time and money—and build a list of warm candidates much faster. That way, instead of building a pool of twenty-two qualified candidates, HR is free to cut that number in half, confident that they already have several strong prospects in the fold.

In scenarios like this, we've seen the lead time for hiring shrink from ten weeks down to three or four, saving companies as much as 50 to 75 percent in recruiting costs in the process. It's easy to think of the cost of advertising, interviewing, and training as fixed, but it doesn't have to be so. Whether your company is thriving or dying, if you can cut your department's workload in half while still producing the same results (in this case, hiring top-notch employees), then that's going to have a massive impact on your bottom line.

MAXIMIZE SALES CAPTURE WITH THE LEAST AMOUNT OF LABOR AND EXPENSE

Here's another apparel example. Imagine a new type of polo shirt came in on the most recent delivery. Aside from the different sizes (small, medium, large, and extra large), you also have twenty-three different colors. With this variety, you have to figure out the best way to distribute to your eight hundred stores. How many of each color and size do you send to each store?

Actually, that's not the only logistics question you have to worry about. You also have to take pictures of all twenty-three different-colored polos for your website, set up twenty-three different items in your system, and create twenty-three different spaces in your warehouse.

That's a lot of work, but imagine if you could capture 95 percent of your potential sales with only seven colors— and by doing so, you'd also cut the labor cost of setup, management, and warehousing by over two-thirds. Would you take that opportunity?

This is another good example of where the art of analytics meets the science. Sure, you're not maximizing sales in this scenario. In fact, you're generating slightly fewer sales, but since it was costing you more than a dollar to capture each of those incremental dollars, that's okay. Instead, you're maximizing your *sales capture* by dramatically reducing your labor and expense. This just goes to show that sometimes sales aren't everything. If you can optimize expenses, then even a slightly smaller amount of revenue ultimately equals more money in your pocket.

MAKE THE BEST DECISION POSSIBLE

There's an old saying: "A person with two watches never knows what time it is." The Telco company, whose story we shared earlier in the chapter, had two watches. One watch told them they had zero open installation orders that exceeded seven days. The other watch told them that more and more customers were getting unhappy as the company improved service. But which was the right answer? Was it the former? The latter? Both?

A good analytics program thrives under the premise that the best decision is the right one, the second-best decision is the wrong one, and the worst decision is no decision. Unfortunately, because so many businesses don't know what they need, they hold off on making any decisions at all. Stuck in an endless loop of analysis paralysis, they just avoid the analytics conversation altogether.

That's the worst decision you can make.

It feels like you didn't decide yet, but no decision was chosen. If you aren't making analytics a part of your business process, then you're already falling behind. As this chapter showed, more is already possible with analytics than you may realize.

With a well-executed analytics program, one in which roles, nomenclature, values, and priorities are properly defined, you'll always know which watch to look at, what it's telling you, and how to respond. In other words, you'll know how to go from making the *worst* decision to the *best*.

Viewed in that light, the question isn't *whether* to start, but rather *how* to start. In the next chapter, you'll learn how to take that first step toward making analytics a core component of your business's decision-making process.

CHAPTER 3

MAKING ANALYTICS A STRATEGIC PRIORITY

We can all agree that a capable CEO is essential to the long-term success of a company. Similarly, we can also agree that a security guard is essential to the day-to-day success of that same company. Both are important, but the nature of their respective jobs is fundamentally different. The former's role is strategic, while the latter's is tactical.

The difference between these two types of roles can be best understood in the role player's absence. For instance, imagine what might happen if your security guard is sick and doesn't show up for work one day. Immediately, chaos ensues. How do you get people in the garage? How do you make sure everybody has the right clearance?

While you're scrambling to answer these questions, all your visitors are backed up trying to get into the lobby, and all around the company people are going crazy and fighting fires.

Now, imagine that your CEO ups and quits without any warning. They just don't show up one day. What happens? People are surprised, and there's plenty of confusion, but the day-to-day operations of the company more or less stay the same. There are no additional fires to fight, no real chaos to speak of.

This isn't to say that your CEO's departure won't cause problems in the long run, of course. It certainly will. But in the short term, the sudden absence of your security guard (the person in the tactical role) is going to have a much greater impact on your day-to-day operations than the sudden absence of your CEO (the person in the strategic role).

In the tactical world, we're constantly fighting fires—receiving emails and texts from people who have to reschedule lunch, or last-minute phone calls declining accepted meeting invites because they're too busy fighting a fire somewhere in their company to make their appointment. It's an easy trap to fall into, but it's also a sure sign that your business isn't behaving as strategically as it could. The more effort you put into thinking about and preparing for the long term—in other words, the more attention you give to strategic planning—the less likely you are to be engaged in tactical fires.

It's easy to think of analytics as a tactical, transactional system, just like our security guard. The reality, however, is that analytics is the exact opposite—it's strategic. It's a long-term play for the health and well-being of your company—which is essential to the survival of your business, but easy to forget through the course of everyday work. However, because many organizations don't treat their analytics programs with the strategic importance they deserve, those programs are often sidelined to the transactional systems in the firefighting world.

Think of investing in analytics the way you invest in a 401(k). If you don't put money into it in your twenties, thirties, or forties, nothing happens. You're perfectly fine in the short term (though your long-term outlook is another story). The strategic need of saving up for retirement has little to no effect on your everyday experience. However, on the tactical side, if you don't set money aside for lunch today, then you're going to be very grouchy— and you're going to drop everything else you're doing to figure out how you're going to get fed.

The firefight of eating lunch today is always going to win out over investing in your retirement for tomorrow.

Similarly, the firefight of a crashed website or a faulty employee time-tracking system is always going to win out over the strategic needs of filing a key analytics report. Heads won't roll if that report isn't updated, but heads *will* roll when your site crashes or your time-tracking system goes offline. The short-term urgency of our tactical needs will always win out over your long-term analytics needs in a firefight.

The solution? Avoid the firefight.

In this chapter, we're going to talk about the value of making analytics a strategic priority in your company by avoiding the transactional methodologies and setting your team up with dedicated resources on a published roadmap. By doing so, you remove your analytics program from the cycle of panic and firefighting that affects so many businesses.

For many, this represents a huge mindset shift, but it's essential to the long-term success of your analytics program. When companies don't take a strategic approach to their analytics program, their efforts are usually lost in the shuffle of everyday business. They start strong, but once they hit their first speed bump, they put the program on the back burner and head off to fight the latest round of daily fires. Remember we know that 80 percent of analytics projects fail; this is just another one of the reasons why.

SHIFTING MINDSET FROM TRANSACTIONAL TO ANALYTICAL

Facts are facts. Data can't be changed. However, your approach to that data *can* change, which in turn can dramatically impact the insights you gain—and often for the better. The key to this is understanding the difference between a transactional approach and an analytical approach.

- **Transactional:** Rote, basic, or systematic—black and white. You specify what you want, and your team member follows your instructions to the letter.
- **Analytical:** Nuanced, holistic, "it depends"—a gray area. You specify what you want, and your team member works to produce results that account for nuances and deviations but that deliver on the *intent* of your request.

Both roles are essential for the health of an organization. However, where many analytics programs struggle is that they put transactional-minded team members in charge of tasks that are better suited for someone with an analytical approach to sniff out any fundamental nuances, like the kinds of nuances we identified in chapter 2.

If you're in a true analytical role, you won't get pulled away for firefighting for transactional assistance. It doesn't matter where in the company you're located;

that's simply not your job. Let the firefighters fight the fires, while you keep your eye on the long-term goals of the company.

To clearly illustrate this difference, let's look at a few examples.

EXAMPLE 1

In one company, the CMO wanted to rank all his active customers. So, he instructed his IT team to stack rank their customers for usage over the past twelve months and then break those groups into 10 percent chunks and sort them from top to bottom. (In statistics, this process is called *deciling*.)

Taking their typical data approach, his transactional systems-focused team followed the CMO's instructions to the letter. They did exactly what he asked: they took all the active customers, summed up their usage over the past twelve months, and stack ranked them. This sounded like it would work, but there was one problem: not all active customers had been using the service for a full twelve months. Some had only been customers for four months, while others had just signed up.

Following the CMO's instructions to the letter was bound to create a host of problems with the data. Someone taking an analytical approach would hear the CMO's instructions, build a model that accounted for all the customers who hadn't yet been with the company for a year, and then weight their data accordingly.

EXAMPLE 2

Next, let's look at the world of billing. In standard billing practices, a company doesn't bill all its customers at once. It bills 10 percent of its customers one day, 10 percent more three days later, and so on. It's why your utility and credit cards bills arrive at different times throughout the month. Invariably, some customers are billed right around the end of one month or the beginning of the next. Depending on exactly how the cycle works, for example, a customer could be billed on January 31, March 1, and then March 31.

These bills each fall a month apart, even if no bills fall in February and two fall in the actual month of March. This is easy enough to understand, but a transactional approach to customer reporting might fail to account for this, rendering the 10 percent of customers whose billing period falls outside of the actual month, by name, all but invisible.

Here, it's important to point out that there are no bad actors in this scenario. It's just a function of the difference between the black-and-white processes of the transactional world and the gray area of the analytical world.

In other words, because of the specific way the code is written and input, an employee might look at the data and think, "These customers are no longer active because they didn't receive a bill in February," which is technically true. Employees like this aren't *intentionally* ignoring those 10 percent of customers. Rather, that 10 percent of customers is lost in the implementation of system-related queries that are very precise in their language—if you specify all customers who were mailed a bill in February, that's what you get.

Once a person becomes *aware* of a nuance like this, then they can account for it in the kinds of queries they write. In fact, once they become aware of enough different kinds of nuances like this, then they will have learned how to step out of the black-and-white mindset of writing code and into the gray-area mindset of a skilled analyst.

GETTING IN THE STRATEGIC MINDSET

If you approach analytics from a transactional approach, you are starting out with a methodology that's the wrong playbook and will gloss over important information, causing crucial insights to be lost. If analytics is strategic rather than tactical, how do you set it up to guarantee success within your business? For the rest of the chapter, we're going to explore a series of important mindset shifts necessary for successful analytics adoption.

ANALYTICS IS NOT BLACK AND WHITE

In a transactional system, the decision-making is already taken care of—it's rote. All you have to do is follow the script. Colloquially, this is known as *paving the cow path.* Historically, when you were looking to build a road, you would just pave over the cow path and call it good. Similarly, when companies have sought to build an analytics program, they've simply automated whatever manual efforts they were already making. This might make good short-term sense, but it fails to ask the question: Is this the path we should be paving over? Is there a better way to approach this?

For instance, the money taken out of your paycheck follows a transactional approach; every penny is accounted for each and every time. Some of it goes to the IRS, some goes into your 401(k), and some goes into your savings. Everything is nice and rote, and there's no question about what you should be doing.

But let's look at your 401(k) a little closer. It's great that you're putting a set amount into your retirement plan every month, but is it enough? How much have you been putting in over the lifetime of your employment? Were you allowed to participate in the company 401(k) during your first year, and if not, how did that affect your contribution?

These are all important questions, and none of them has an easy answer. Instead of answers being black and white like they are in a transactional system, they are gray—and usually a little different for every employee. Some may be putting in enough money into their 401(k), while others may not. There are many variables to consider, which requires a good deal of strategic thinking.

This also means that analytics requires active thinking and constant decision-making. In that way, it's very different from rote work. You can't just set up a series of rules, automate them, and call it good. You have to consider what your goals are and what the best approach might be to realizing those goals.

ANALYTICS SHOULD BE DIRECTLY TIED TO VALUE

You don't want your business support staff or IT project manager to be the owner of your analytics effort. Nor do you want your business intelligence representative to be the owner. Instead, you want an executive sponsor in charge of the project, somebody who has actual P&L responsibility. Having an executive sponsor in place as the project owner will help ensure that your analytics efforts are value driven and tied to specific business goals.

Many businesses don't put an executive sponsor in charge as the project owner. As a result, they don't see any results. A tool jockey is skilled in optimizing how a tool is used. That's not the same as knowing what information to include. How is that system going to drive value in the enterprise? Creativity is good, but creativity with a *goal* is better. A P&L-responsible executive sponsor as project owner will keep the focus not just on building a good system but one that is directly tied to monetizing your data.

LIMIT OR MANAGE BIAS

Imagine you own a chain of thirty sporting goods stores. Of those, five stores have seen a steady, predictable decline in sales. They're not hitting the margins they were hoping to, and spending more on marketing and other means hasn't produced any significant revenue.

From all the information available, the smart insight would be to close the stores and focus on strengthening the performance of the other twenty-five. You see these numbers and you know that closing these stores might be in your company's best interests, but you don't want to follow through. After all, one of those stores was the original shop on which you grew your entire business. Another store is run by one of your good friends, who you don't want to be out of a job. From your perspective, each of these five stores has a good reason why it should stay open, despite what the data says. From another perspective, someone whose job is analyzing store performance, closing the stores would be a no-brainer. However, you just can't bring yourself to do it.

Because the data is telling you something you don't want to hear, you choose to ignore it.

This is a common tendency among us humans, whether in business, politics, or even recreation. In poker, for instance, when someone becomes emotional (usually after taking a bad beat), they are no longer able to stick to their strategy. They're now playing *on tilt,* which leads to weaker, irrational decision-making—and suboptimal results. Whatever our perspective, whatever we're incentivized to believe, we often choose to believe despite what the numbers may tell us. The problem is that the more biased you are in this way, the weaker results you will produce.

The question is, how do we combat this tendency? How do we put ourselves into a mindset where we are able to take the data at face value and use it to make the best decisions for our business? We'll get more into this discussion in later chapters, but for now, here's the bottom line: If you feel like you already know the answer, there's nothing to be gained from further information because you've already made up your mind. However, if you don't believe you know the answer or if you're open to hearing other opportunities, the data has a lot to tell. When you understand that your perspective within an organization colors what you think is important or correct, you're that much more likely to act in a way that benefits the organization rather than supports your own opinions.

AVOID THE FIREFIGHT AT ALL COSTS

When it comes to analytics, you have to strategically set yourself up for success. If you don't do that, your analytics effort will fail. Analytics is a long-term game that is equal parts art and science. While analytics is an A priority when it comes to strategy, it is a C priority when it comes to tactical requirements—the nonurgent work of analytics is going to lose out to the urgent work of transactional system firefighting every time—no matter how much importance you put on the program.

But here's the good news: while you can't win in a firefight, you *can* avoid the firefight altogether.

To refresh from chapter 1, the concepts of data, information, and insights exist on a continuum. Data are just the facts, unambiguous, and not to be debated. Information converts that data into something useful in the real world. Finally, insights are the conclusions and actions you take with the information available to you.

To put this into the real world, let's go back to the story of our energy retailer from chapter 2. It was a fact that the retailer had two hundred thousand accounts. That data would never change. The information we derived from that data was that, while the company had two hundred thousand accounts, they only had thirty-five thousand distinct customers. Finally, our insight was that if the company focused on the top 10 percent of those thirty-five thousand customers, they could capture an additional $100 million in revenue with just a twelve-person team.

Analytics intelligence helps you to turn this data into information, and information into actionable insights that will allow you to monetize your business. Analysts have many tools at their disposal to make this happen, but working with data will always be part science, and part art. The data may never change, but how we look at it does. This is why it's so important to (a) put strategic, rather than transactional thinkers in front of the data, and (b) tie your analytics efforts to clear, value-driven business goals of someone with P&L responsibility.

ANALYTICS IN ACTION

Dollar General was growing like mad—often opening three, four, even five new stores every single day. With that many stores, better demand forecasting could be a huge difference maker. Imagine reducing overstocks (wasted inventory carrying costs) and eliminating the "holes" (item stockouts which drives missed sales) for over ten thousand stores. That could be a gigantic financial win, but how to scale to that degree?

We began by normalizing the merchandise replenishment methods. Previously, we essentially reordered what was sold. But now we wanted to automate and smarten up the reordering. By feeding key data—such as promotional activity, seasonality, number of stores reordering the product, and other items bought in the market basket—into machine learning algorithms, we could begin to automate the reordering quantities.

Once we were able to optimize and take advantage of that data, we poured in more key attributes to not just fine-tune the reordering, but also to optimize the individual store's weekly run from one of seventeen distribution centers (DCs). This step required better understanding of that store's unique fingerprint (e.g., proximity to a big box retail alternative, demographics of the store's surrounding population).

With all of this information now cleansed and codified, by optimizing the pick and pack for each store and optimizing the drive route, we reduced the truck miles driven from the DC to complete the store's weekly replenishment. What a success! In the end, we were able to achieve a 2 percent sales increase on over $24 billion in revenue by increasing needed stock by the 12 percent that allowed filling the holes on the shelves. Additionally, we experienced a 28 percent reduction on safety stock excess in DCs and captured a 1 percent shrink reduction by not having excess stock in the back of the stores that usually is an easy target for shrink.

—Bobby Aflatooni, formerly VP, IT supply chain and operations, Dollar General. Currently, SVP, infrastructure, Howard Hughes Corporation

For your analytics efforts to work, you have to set them up correctly up front, which means:

- Transactional team members can't be in charge. They'll get pulled off to fight fires.
- The project owner must be clearly identified. And it must be someone with P&L responsibility.
- Value being targeted must be specific. And it should directly benefit the project owner's P&L area.
- Everybody needs to be on the same page. Consensus understanding of gray is harder than black and white.

Failure to follow these basic tenets results in infighting among your team. Unfortunately, this is precisely what happens to the many organizations that attempt to set up an analytics program without a clear plan.

For this reason, perhaps more than any other, analytics success is elusive. However, when set up correctly with clearly defined roles and value-driven goals, you are guaranteed to generate results and boost your bottom line.

Many businesses aren't prepared for the day-in, day-out commitment that a successful analytics program brings. They'll be full of energy and enthusiasm in the beginning, but eventually their attention and interest wanes. Perhaps they have too many fires to put out, or perhaps they felt overwhelmed by the amount of work they had to put in. Whatever the case, they eventually lose steam—and eventually so does their program.

In part 2, you'll learn how to lay the groundwork for long-term analytics success. As you move through the next section, remember: The hard work of analytics isn't sexy. Just like dieting, saving money, or exercising, the basic principles aren't complex. Executing it, however, is challenging and takes daily commitment—and a clear understanding of the value your program can bring.

PART 2

LAYING THE GROUNDWORK

CHAPTER 4

BUILDING YOUR ANALYTICS FOUNDATION

Imagine you work for a retail company. Your company has thirty different buyers, people who select and purchase different merchandise for your stores. Individually, your buyers all do fine work, but collectively, there's just one problem: they all calculate the company's margin on what they buy in a slightly different way.

Naturally, having thirty different ways to calculate margin isn't helpful to anyone, since it means that no one is clear on precisely what the other team members are doing.[5] As the manager of this group, now that you've identified the problem, you have a couple options:

---

5. And over time, without standardization, I can promise you that the most uniquely beneficial calculation for each buying office will prevail, artificially inflating results.

1. Pick the best definition of margin among your thirty team members to standardize on impacts all but one buying office, leaving the other twenty-nine unhappy.
2. Formulate a new best practice definition of calculating margin and standardize everyone to it. Now, all buying offices are impacted and potentially thirty of your team members may be unhappy.

How Do We Calculate Margin?

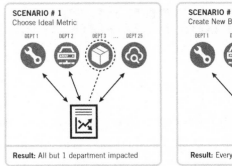

No matter which path we choose, there will be impact to BAU (Business As Usual).

From the get-go, no matter which of these options you take, you're not set up for there to be much happiness, adoption, or consensus for how to calculate margin. It's not easy getting thirty people on the same page. Everyone has their own way they like to do things, and most people are generally resistant to change unless they have a good reason to do so.

If that sounds bleak, here's the good news. The more

effort you put into defining the roles, processes, and terminology of your analytics program at the beginning, the less likely you are to encounter challenges like this down the road. To do that, you'll want to set up a strong core team of key players and decision-makers to oversee your analytics efforts.

In this chapter, we'll discuss how to build a strong foundation within your business so that your analytics program can thrive. A strong foundation begins with strong governance—a system in which the few represent the many. Driving this effort are your core/project team, your executive/steering committee and your governance council, who work to establish a common lexicon, determine priorities, and provide central validation. As you read through these practices, remember that components like these aren't optional—they're essential. If you and your key stakeholders aren't on the same page from the outset, your analytics program will likely face challenges almost immediately.

WHAT IS GOVERNANCE?

In chapter 2, we told the story of the dating service that had a problem with understanding the data from its campaign relative to the different time zones in which they ran. As they discovered, the midnight cutoff point they had been using effectively made them blind to all the valuable data they were collecting for their West Coast audience.

While it was good the dating service had discovered the problem, they still needed to come up with a solution that everyone agreed upon. This was no small task. One group wanted to set the new cutoff at four hours after the ad dropped, another wanted to set it at six hours, while still another wanted to set it at three.

Luckily, the dating service had the foresight to create a defined project team responsible for solving problems just like this one. This team was able to look at the problem, come up with a solution that fit everyone's needs, and then make sure that everyone was in agreement.

Solving for problems across teams and departments often results in infighting, redundancies, and inconsistent approaches to your data collection and analysis. This is a big waste of time and money—and it doesn't produce a result.

The project team gets everybody on the same page, proposes a solution that accounts for everybody's needs, and ensures that everybody moves forward together. For this reason, a properly staffed project team is essential to the long-term success of any analytics effort.

THE IMPORTANCE OF COMMON GOVERNANCE

Imagine that you own a chain of gas stations. Each has a convenience store and fuel pumps to sell gasoline. You're interested in determining how much gasoline you sell per fuel pump across locations, but as you go to collect the data, you realize that each team at each location has its own way of representing the information.

- One team breaks down the pumps into islands with two islands at their location, they say they have two fuel pumps.
- Another team presents the information in terms of card-reading machines; they also have two islands, but since they have two card-reading machines per island, they say they have four fuel pumps.
- Still another team argues that it's not just a matter of card-reading machines but also a matter of fuel type and blend. Each machine distributes regular, mid-premium, and premium gas and/or diesel—meaning each should be its own pump. With the mix of options offered, they list their fuel pump count at ten.

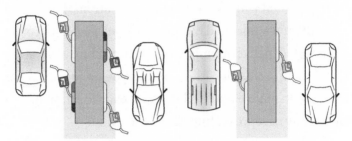

Unique and compelling answers could include two pumps, four pumps, six pumps, and even ten pumps. That creates up to four variations of the same mathematical metric; comparing "fuel sales by pump" across locations would result in apples and oranges comparisons.

So, what constitutes a fuel pump? Even for stations with the same number of islands, the same number of card-reading machines, and the same number of fuel choices per dispensing handle, the only difference is how each team has chosen to define the term. So, any reporting on gasoline you are selling by fuel pump across locations will be meaningless.

Without proper governance in place, issues like this will go unsolved—and then spiral into a much bigger problem when it comes time to assemble your data into information. By that point, it will be clear that nobody's numbers line up with the documented calculations, but nobody will be sure why. The effort required to go back, work with each individual team, identify the discrepancy, and verify the numbers with every constituency would be prohibitively expensive and will stop your analytics efforts dead in their tracks. The more teams reporting to you, the greater this problem becomes.

Establishing a basic governance model is essential to the long-term success of your analytics program. The following considerations will help guide you as you begin to lay the foundation for your team.

THE BUCK STOPS WITH THE PROJECT OWNER

The purpose of the project team, or the core team, is to deliver the best analytics results. To ensure that they are doing their job correctly, the project leader reports findings and decisions to the executive sponsor, the project owner. That way, all goals and their measurable values (see chapter 6) have clear focus and a direct line to monetizing your efforts.

DEFINE ROLES AND RESPONSIBILITIES BEFOREHAND

We once worked with a company where the business team would say, "IT is terrible. They can never deliver on time."

Meanwhile the IT team would say, "The business side is crazy. They can't even make up their mind about what they want."

Like anything, both complaints had some legitimacy, but the truth likely lay somewhere in the middle. Unfortunately, neither had any interest in finding that middle ground, which led to a mess of delays and timeline issues. IT would promise delivery on a project by late June, and business would agree.

Then, in another meeting two weeks later, a critically important member of the business team would come back and say, "I'm at a conference at the end of June. We're going to have to push this deadline back."

This angered the IT team to no end. If this business team couldn't stick to a deadline, then why was IT being blamed for all the delays?

It was clear that before we helped build out this company's analytics efforts, we would have to sit down with them and establish a basic set of ground rules. Otherwise, the two teams would never be able to work together. For every scenario we could game out, an appropriate process and response would already be in place. If a member from the business team couldn't make a meeting, for instance, they would send an informed proxy to the meeting instead so that IT could preserve their timeline. On the flipside, if IT had a promised delivery date, they would not push it back because of another project's strategic needs or unexpected emergency system fix without first discussing alternatives with the business team.

If you come up with the rules after the fact, then it's easy to point fingers and blame the other for not upholding their end of the bargain. However, if everyone comes into a project with set protocols to follow, then everyone is happier—and everything is much more likely to get done.

ESTABLISH A COMMON LEXICON

If you're going to collect and analyze your data successfully, everyone has to work from the same definition. Every single person working with this information must know what is meant by a fuel pump. Is it the island/dog bone? Is it the card-reading machine? Is it the fuel grade options? Is it none of the above?

A common nomenclature solves this problem. In fact, a properly developed new lexicon wouldn't even use the term "fuel pump." Why? First, no one knows how many literal mechanical fuel pumps there are underground, and that fact is irrelevant anyway. Second, doing so is confusing; with so many working definitions of the term *fuel pump* that the mere mention of it pulls people offside.

Instead, use a lexicon that leaves no ambiguity: terms like *fueling islands, dispensing sides, fuel nozzles, product offerings,* and *gasoline octane grade offerings.* Those terms are easy to understand, unambiguous, and easy to count.

Example of a Good, Common, and Enhanced Metric List

Note: there is no definition for the metric representing the 10 product offering choices summed across dispensing side as that metric has no real actionable value in the business.

ALLOW THE FEW TO REPRESENT THE MANY

If you need consensus from your team of thirty departments for every decision you make, you're not going to get very much done—but you're going to spend a lot of time (and therefore money) doing it. From an ROI perspective, is it really worth the cost of having thirty people sit in on every governance council meeting? Probably not.

Instead, let the few represent the many. Identify a few of your top-performing team members who you trust to do the right thing—folks who others look up to. If, for any reason, they can't make a meeting on a given day, don't wait to reschedule. Each team member will have an informed proxy who will sit in for them when necessary. That way, your analytics program is far more likely to stay both on time and on budget.

Aside from improving decision-making, smaller groups also improve participation among team members. After all, what feels more important: sitting on a team of thirty or sitting on a team of five? The smaller the group, the greater the sense of exclusivity—and therefore responsibility. This makes it more likely for your team members to commit to and make time for meetings, as they know that any absence will be noticed, and their contributions will be missed.

If you're one of thirty and represent only your department, your contributions won't feel that important. However, if you're one of five who represents and speaks on behalf of twenty-five other departments, you know that your role is important, which in and of itself adds greater weight to your participation.

PROVIDE CENTRAL VALIDATION

In the opening story to this chapter, we saw thirty buyers with thirty competing definitions for how to calculate margin. To address the issue, the governance council sets a new definition, tests and validates it, and holds all teams accountable to that standard.

Inevitably when this happens, someone on one of the teams is either going to be unhappy or they're going to disagree with your method of calculation. "I don't like that number," they say. "I came up with something different."

At this point, you have two options:

1. Assign a team to take a deep dive into their numbers to understand what they came up with, which will take at least three weeks.
2. Validate your calculation again using your centralized definition and correct if necessary.

The first option is going to take loads of labor hours and is unlikely to leave you any better off than you were before. The second option provides a centralized standard that all teams can be held accountable to, and it insulates you against any pushback from cranky team members. All calculations are created centrally and distributed for management and knowledge workers to use and, therefore, everybody is working off of the same information.

ESTABLISH AN ANALYTICS SPECIALIST

Business folks and tech folks talk differently.

Tech folks tend to be more direct: "Tell me exactly what you want and we'll build it."

Business folks tend to be more circuitous: "I can't tell you exactly what I want, but I can tell you if I like it when I see it."

This difference in communication and conceptualization inevitably leads to problems. How can the tech team build to something that hasn't been properly defined? As far as the business folks are concerned, that's not their problem—unless of course the tech team comes back several months later with something they don't like.

This is why we recommend establishing a business/tech liaison, or what we refer to as an *analytics specialist*. This hybrid resource is able to listen to their business or tech associates, understand both the specifics and the intent of their request, and communicate it to the other party in a way that is clear and actionable.

Think back to that energy retailer from chapter 2. At one point, the tech team was tasked with creating a report of all their active customers following a monthly billing cycle. The tech team delivered exactly that—but this created a problem: all the customers who were billed around the end of the month (about 10 percent of their customer base) were eliminated from the report.

Through no fault of their own, the tech team's technical query hadn't accounted for the nuances of the CMO's request. These missing 10 percent of customers were still active, but because of where they fell on the billing cycle, their invoices read January 31, March 1, and March 31. Yes, they had received a bill for the February billing *cycle*, but they had not actually been mailed an invoice bill in the literal month of February.

This example shows the difference between the literal question and the real question. A well-trained analytics specialist understands the difference between the two and is able to approach their work in a way that satisfies the needs of all parties. Were the CMO to deliver the same request to the analytics specialist, that person would have translated the request to the tech team accordingly instead of taking the instruction literally and executing only against that.

Analytics specialists know how the data is meant to be interpreted and don't view it as just bits and bytes of data. This knowledge is invaluable when it comes time to convert the data from information and then to insights. Few have the well-honed ability to understand both the intent of the effort and take the steps necessary to turn that data into useful information.

So where do you find the kind of person capable of performing this task? Most often, it's someone who's been around the analytics block more than a couple times—

specifically a person who comes from a pure analytics, or a data-focused, company. They've participated in, or perhaps even managed, various analytics projects and are familiar with the kinds of errors likely to come up and what approaches they can take to neutralize them. In fact, that's how they came to be an analytics specialist in the first place: they've experienced this scenario and two dozen others like it, and they know how to adjust accordingly. Having a specialist like this will save you from making those same two dozen errors because you didn't know to look for them.

Companies like Facebook, Google, and Frito-Lay who have actively built a culture around data already have these kinds of business/tech liaisons in place. Most other companies do not. Which means they're left to identify employees with hidden talents among their ranks, hire someone new for the role, or contract with a third-party analytics provider.

PREPARE FOR TEST DAY

In school, most people are rarely surprised by the results of an exam. Long before the test is handed out, you know exactly how well prepared you are (or aren't), and your score will usually reflect that.

ANALYTICS IN ACTION

Back in 2006, the big players in coolers, such as Igloo, Coleman, and Rubbermaid, had evolved into a business that was simply driven off volume, which translated into a price-only focus. This left a huge void in the market for a high-quality cooler, one that was worth owning.

Since the founding of YETI, everything we cared about was value—value to the end consumer and, similarly, value to the customer/retailer. Even though our initial product offerings were priced ten times that of the ordinary cooler, that premium made sense because it drove tremendous value to the consumer via lifestyle enhancement and product desirability. In the same vein, it offered tremendous value to the customer/retailer too: "Why try to compete with Walmart selling $30 coolers and keeping the $5 margin when you can sell a $300 cooler and keep $100?"

As business heated up, when we sat down to do the annual channel resets, we had to think about information with a strategic long-term view, not just reacting to the most recent short-term results. For example, the data showed that we had lots of really good retailers that paid on time and moved a lot of product. But our gut said not all sales are the same. For example, internet sellers with no real customer following were simply one-time transactions, so the lifetime value of that consumer was low. Similarly, a large grocery chain moved a lot of volume, but we believed the consumer discovery point was key and that the initial experience drove overall long-term product desirability. And discovering a new product was not the same consumer experience across all channels, so a lifestyle shop or high-end hardware store should actually deliver better long-term results.

As we followed this strategy of overweighting channel results based on the consumer journey, the underlying evidence shown by repeat purchases and increased consumer loyalty proved out our core beliefs. It was true—not all sales are the same.

—Ryan Seiders, co-founder, YETI Coolers

Building an analytics program works the same way. If you don't prepare for success ahead of time, you have no reason to suspect that things will go well. On the other hand, if you are diligent, if you clearly define your needs, responsibilities, and goals—and if you put in the proper foundation to support that—you have every reason to expect that you will succeed.

At this point, you're still only in the early stages of building your program, but make no mistake: this is a make-or-break moment.

When building the foundation of your analytics program, it's not good enough to adopt only *some* of these practices. We've found that if even one of these considerations is absent, the risk of failure dramatically increases—think of a chain and how it is only as strong as its weakest link. Considering that the likelihood of analytics success is already low—again, only between 20 and 30 percent—you need every advantage you can get.

In other words, to get different results, you have to do things differently.

These are the essential foundational steps necessary to make your analytics program work and help you accomplish what you set out to do. Take your time with this step, and make sure that you've covered all your bases. Once you've done that, then you and your team can begin to establish the goals and values that will give your program the focus and clarity necessary to thrive.

CHAPTER 5

ESTABLISHING WHERE YOU ARE

Imagine that you're a fitness instructor in charge of training one of your clients for a marathon. In order to set up the right program for your client, you first have to understand some basic facts about who they are and where they are in their fitness goals:

- Are they in good physical shape?
- Have they participated in athletic events in their life before?
- Are they overweight?
- Do they have a good diet?
- Do they have a sedentary lifestyle?
- Have they run races in the past?
- Have they ever run before?

The same basic process applies to your analytics program. In order to reach your end state—in other words, to achieve your goals—you must first determine where you are right now:

- Do you know where your data exists?
- Do you know who would use information to develop insights?
- Do you know what actions will be taken to change your business?
- Is there trust in facts and data within the company?
- Does the executive's opinion matter more than data?

Wherever you are, something is likely holding you back from achieving your goal. Your goal is to discover what it is that's holding you back so that you can build the right roadmap for moving forward. Often, this problem falls along one of three lines:

- **Organizational.** The interdepartmental people that need to be involved and whether they are in alignment.
- **Cultural.** Some organizations care about the art of analytics (using data to drive business decisions), while others only care about the art of their business (using their gut to make business decisions). If a company isn't interested in the facts, then any analytics effort would be pointless.

- **Technological.** Do you have the infrastructure it takes to implement what's needed?

Whatever the case, it's important that you understand this problem and address it before moving forward.

To give an example, let's say you set out to rate your company's readiness for adopting an analytics program. On a scale of one to ten, you determine that your tech and your org are each at a full ten—meaning those aspects of your business are ready to go—but your culture is only at a three. Following this, if you want to adopt a thriving analytics program, your first job is to focus on culture and make sure everybody is on board with the program objectives and team structures, give extra attention to adoption management, and not treat change management as an afterthought.

All this raises an important question: How do you assess where you are right now? There are many ways to approach this, but the following questions will help you begin to assess your analytics readiness from a variety of standpoints within your organization.

ORGANIZATIONAL/BUSINESS

Q: Is there a significant gap between management consensus and the individual contributor-level con-

sensus regarding actual reporting and analytics usage?

For example, senior management might claim that everybody has specific reports that they use every day for at least an hour. However, when you ask individual knowledge workers if this is true, they say, "We never use those reports. They don't work."

Q: Do the A priorities greatly outweigh all the B and C priorities?

In other words, is everything an A priority? If so, there is likely an organizational issue from the business side.

ORGANIZATIONAL/TECHNOLOGY

Q: Does the corporate IT group want to assign transaction system infrastructure people to the data warehouse and analytics projects without adding additional training?

Bringing the transactional team members without any additional training doesn't tend to work.

Q: Is the technology group unable to define the actual project resources by name and level of time commitment, being number of hours per week?

If these commitments aren't clearly defined, then team members are likely to be pulled off the project to fight fires elsewhere.

SCOPE MANAGEMENT

Q: Are there more than twenty-five named users expected in the initial soft rollout?

If so, that's going to raise a lot of risk. The initial pilot needs to be a soft launch before rolling out to the masses. You don't want a whole bunch of people involved.

Q: Is the reporting system update frequently required at a more granular level than daily?

Everybody wants to jump to real-time reporting because it's a shiny new ball (see chapter 7). However, if you're not taking advantage of the data you're getting weekly and daily, that real-time data will only introduce new problems.

ANALYTICS CULTURE

Q: How hard is it going to be to get good implementation success?

Imagine an executive saying, "I don't see what's so hard

about these analytics systems. I have an analyst that creates this exact same thing in Excel." If your exec is already saying they don't think enterprise analytics is complex, that's a real problem. To put it in perspective, would it make sense to tell the head of supply chain at a package delivery company, "I don't see what's so hard about your job, I can pack my own box to ship something and that's not that hard."

Q: Would users pick illegible abbreviations in report columns because that's "what they are used to?"

Say that a column says "FRCST SLS N30D." Are you able to tell that means "forecasted sales next thirty days?" When you see users doing this, it's usually a sign they're trying to add more and more data to a report as opposed to focusing on the information that's actually needed.

Q: Is there a culture that can utilize information from an analytics perspective?

Or, are they going to be stymied into analysis paralysis, assembling and playing with data or resistant to being data driven?

WHAT'S YOUR RISK?

After we've determined where a client is with respect

to these questions, we then assess the organization's risk factors to implementation.[6] Because we know how difficult analytics projects can be, we want to ensure success—which means being aware of the speed bumps.

Here are the three risk areas that we assess:

- **Delivery risk.** The risk to a successful delivery and user adoption.
- **Timing risk.** The risk to the project timeline. If a project isn't on time, people lose attention and it gets pushed out further.
- **Cost risk.** The ability to stay on budget.

Through our assessment, we determine which of these three factors is going to be the biggest obstacle to successful implementation. Wherever that risk is determines our approach. For example,

- In the case of a delivery risk, we know that client will require more hand-holding, governance, and management updates and communication.
- In the case of a timing risk, say on the organizational business side, we know that we need to get an idea of who our dedicated team members will be and make sure that they buy into the informed proxy concept.

---

6. Please note that these are only a sample/subset of the questions we ask as part of the onboarding process in order to assess analytics readiness.

- In the case of a cost risk, say scope management isn't contained, we would work with the client to have their A, B, and C priorities clearly defined and differentiated in a way that everybody understands and agrees to.

None of these risks is better or worse than the other. Rather, it's all about *knowing* what the risks are so that you can come up with an effective game plan. Just as in football you might want to build a strategy around your opponent's devastating running game, in analytics, you want to know the organizational challenges you face so that you account for them effectively.

DECIDE WHERE YOU WANT TO BE

Now that you know where you are, it's time to define where you want to go.

You probably already have an idea of this, even if you haven't ever formally sat down to think about it. Most likely, it's the thing about your business that you worry the most about, the fear or desire that keeps you up at night. For instance:

- Your competitors are stealing your business.
- You don't know how to hire fast enough to support your growth.

- You're churning through customers and you don't know why.

If major concerns like this aren't keeping you up at night, instead think about what you're spending most of your time on.

That said, just because you're spending a lot of time on something doesn't mean you're doing so effectively. For instance, many organizations spend far too much time assembling data and not enough time interpreting data. Both are important, but the former can be automated; let your computers do what they were made to do—that is, unless your job description reads, "Fool around with data all day long, and don't make any insights."

Remember the big picture. Your goal is to monetize your business by changing an action. But no action is going to be changed if you're spending 80 percent of your time assembling data and 20 percent analyzing it. If you're spending too much of your time in the wrong place, then one of your goals will likely be to flip these numbers so that you and your team are freed up to engage with your data, convert it to useful information, generate insights, and monetize your business.

ANALYTICS IN ACTION

What if you had a hyper-aware virtual observer objectively overseeing your key activities? Imagine how well labor could be aligned so production and service levels perfectly matched customer demand. We operate 132 Price Chopper/Market 32 supermarkets, many including full-service delis and prepared foods service stations. Sometimes we roast too many chickens for the store's daily needs (the overage gets thrown away and categorized as shrink), and other times we understaff the sliced meats counter and disappoint customers (a lost sales opportunity).

Enter the future: recent beaconing technology, such as Wi-Fi and Bluetooth, allows awareness of mobile device location and movement to within three meters. But emerging radar frequency technology improves customer movement tracking accuracy to within ten centimeters, which creates a lot of data, but is a game changer for foot traffic analysis. We can observe precise customer journey movements through a store—what aisles did they walk, which products did they spend time considering, and which products were ultimately purchased?

More specifically, we can understand when customers visit the prepared foods/deli section. Typically more traffic means more sales, but if a customer "dwells" too long around the deli counter and isn't able to get what they want, that's a problem. Is she perturbed by slow service (decreased customer satisfaction), or is she so frustrated that she abandons the experience (lost sales)?

When patterns in body movement tracking correlate to aberrations in sales for deli counter items, we can potentially identify self-fulfilling unproductive labor forecasts based on low sales history and trend. Foot traffic analysis may support adding more labor to a service area even if the sales projection suggests not to. Similarly, by parameterizing the eight-foot sandwich section's traffic, food service production volumes might also be increased to better reflect latent customer demand indicated by foot traffic analysis.

—Sam Wagar, VP, information technology at Golub Corporation/Price Chopper Supermarkets

CHAPTER 6

SETTING GOALS AS VALUES

If you don't have a defined goal, how are you ever going to reach it?

Most people understand this basic premise. However, equally important is defining not only your goals but also defining your goals in terms of *value*—that is, the tangible, real-world benefit that your analytics effort might bring to your business.

Salespeople are great at this. They know that if they can clearly define the value of their product or service, they can persuade more people to buy their product or service. Features are lovely, of course, but it's what those features do for you that matters. For example:

FEATURE-BASED EXAMPLE	VALUE-BASED EXAMPLE
This car gets great gas mileage.	"You will save so much money in fuel." Or, "Imagine how much less you will be impacting the environment."
Tasty ice cream.	"Blue Bell is a best friend, a sad movie, and a good cry."
A great place to vacation that's not too far away.	"The most impressive adventure of your life is in Mexico."
A well-designed and meticulously built timepiece.	"You never actually own a Patek Philippe. You merely look after it for the next generation."

While these are consumer values—business values will be more numbers driven—the concept works the same way. This is the kind of approach you're looking to create with your analytics program.

To achieve your analytics goals, you must clearly define the value that you and your company will capture as a result of it. If you don't define that up front, then two things are likely to happen:

1. That value is going to be really hard to achieve.
2. You're going to lose focus of the big picture and become distracted by the minutiae of the program (or something else entirely).

That second risk is no small matter. We've seen countless analytics efforts become derailed by good, old-fashioned lack of focus. Without the guiding light that a clearly defined value can offer, employees become distracted by the different features of their software, such as the volume of the data, their ability to draft cool reports, neat-looking interactive maps, number of users, and so one. All of those may be nice things, but again, they're features, not value.

This isn't an easy shift for everyone. It's not even an easy shift for *us*, and we know better. The team at Armeta Analytics includes a bunch of engineers. We *love* cool new features and often run the risk of getting distracted by them (especially since we're the ones who get to design them). However, luckily we were also careful to clearly define our value in the early going so that every time we get sucked down a features rabbit hole, we're able to look at the big picture and pull ourselves out of it.

In this chapter, we're going to talk about the importance of establishing goals as values, and how to go about doing it. The best goals are objective, are obtainable, are measurable, have consensus buy-in, and are easily repeatable. Bad goals, on the other hand, speak to features, functions, and abstractions.

Good goals, then, aren't feature focused. They're *value* focused. This distinction is important because if your reasons for setting a goal are arbitrary or only speak to bells and whistles, you and your team may not feel especially motivated to try and reach them. A value-driven purpose behind those goals, on the other hand, can do wonders for your decision-making, focus, and execution.

TURNING GOALS INTO VALUE STATEMENTS

"Be nicer" might sound like a good goal at first, but think for a moment: How would you achieve that? Does being nicer mean giving someone presents? Does it mean complimenting others more? Or does it simply mean showing more courtesy in day-to-day interactions? How would one know they have achieved the goal?

To create good goals, it's useful to first consider the value statement that drives them. To illustrate this concept, let's first start with a bad value statement:

We want the best set of reports for our marketing department that could ever exist.

The second you read this, alarms should be going off. This statement is vague, the goal isn't attainable, and the focus is all feature driven. While these problems are readily apparent when we see them in print, many organizations have grown all too accustomed to creating these exact kinds of vague, shoddy value statements.

To create a better example, let's begin by defining the

problem a little bit better. First, ask the question: Why should it matter how good the reports are that you deliver to your marketing people? What does it matter to them?

The answer is that your marketing department has a problem. Your team has been working a good deal of overtime lately to try and stay on top of their considerable workload. This in turn is diminishing employees' quality of life and contributing to employee churn—none of which is ideal.

Seeing this problem, you craft a value statement that reads:

Improve employees' lives and reduce churn by providing them with reports that allow them to do their job more effectively.

In some ways, this and the original statement may sound similar—they are, after all, both centered around delivering reports. But in reality, they're not similar at all. The second statement doesn't want to deliver "the best set of reports that could ever exist." It wants to deliver reports that help employees do their jobs more effectively. Further, the second statement has a *purpose* behind it (improving lives and reducing churn), while the initial statement has none.

The following table gives you a few more examples of the difference between good goals and bad goals.

FEATURE-DRIVEN GOALS (POOR)	VALUE-DRIVEN GOALS (GOOD)
To deploy a self-service reporting portal.	To reduce 80 percent of the analysts' time spent assembling data (so that they can spend more time on strategic decision-making).
To implement the best HR reporting system.	To be able to accurately identify and track "rising star" employees. To implement reporting that ensures the rising stars are meaningfully engaged by management within every sixty days.
To capture as much data as possible.	To improve employee satisfaction of data scientists by making each workday better and more productive.
To implement a world-class neural network algorithm.	To improve email campaigns by 10 percent without sweetening the offers.
To deploy a visualization tool with drill-anywhere capability.	To make product merchants more productive with vendors when they got to market so that a 5 percent increase in product breadth can be handled without adding additional head count.

Now that you've seen some examples, it's time to build some value statements of your own. For the rest of the chapter, we'll work through some key considerations to help you make your value statements as strong, specific, and repeatable as possible.

DEVELOP A LIST OF OPPORTUNITIES

Imagine you're back at the general store from chapter 1. Among your many other responsibilities, you want to make sure your employees don't quit. You value their work, for one, and you also don't want to go through the hassle of finding another employee with such a limited pool to draw from.

Not all your employees are the same, meaning you can't use the same approach to retain each one. So, you sit down, think about each employee, and come up with an opportunity for each one. For one of your younger employees, you give him a pocketknife that you know he'd like. For the older gentleman working the counter, you give him a walking cane because you know he could use the extra support some days. For another employee, you might give him a paid day off so he can head to the city and take care of some important family business. As a caring business owner, you're always engaged in identifying opportunities like this, if it means retaining your employees and keeping them happy.

HR staff often wrestle with the same issue, albeit on a much larger scale. When grappling with the goal of reducing employee churn by nudging employee satisfaction up by two points, they know that a one-size-fits-all approach won't work. Instead, they identify a list of opportunities that will help them meet that goal:

1. Reach out to your top performers every sixty days to

keep them engaged in the company and make them feel like they matter.

2. Give employees gifts that reflect their knowledge and interests.

3. Provide company-sponsored, family-inclusive events that deepen inter-employee relationships.

As another example, imagine you work in retail, where your specific goal is to increase revenue by 4 percent. To reach that goal, you identify three opportunities:

1. Adding one more item to every five baskets (a 1.2 percent increase in revenue).

2. Increasing foot traffic to your stores during special events (another 0.8 percent increase in revenue).

3. Moving customers toward more premium-level products (a 2 percent increase in revenue).

Add those all up, and you've got your 4 percent total revenue increase.

Finally, let's round things out with one last example from the world of hospitality. Your goal is to increase yield at your hotel—meaning you want as few empty rooms as possible. To reach that goal, you identify three opportunities:

1. Increase the length of stay by one day for every ten reservations.

2. Increase traffic to your website by 13 percent.
3. Sell more packaged deals (e.g., stay for two nights, and dinner is on us the second night).

No matter your industry or your department within a company, it's in your best interest to identify multiple paths toward reaching that same goal.

LET VALUE DRIVE YOUR GOALS

When it comes to crafting good goals, it's essential that you move away from features and function and toward statements that are specific, actionable, and repeatable—in other words, value driven.

For instance, it wouldn't make sense for the general store owner to make this goal, "I want more products in my store." That's a feature, not a goal, and they're smart enough to know that adding more products isn't really what they're after.

Instead, the general store owner's value-driven goal would be more focused. "I want my customers to say that we have the best product selection out there." The general store owner knows this statement is directly tied to value, since achieving it would help the company in several ways:

- It would increase sales.
- It would capture a greater share of customers' wallets.
- It would encourage customers to visit more frequently.

Similarly, the general store owner wouldn't be concerned about having the biggest store out there, as having the biggest store out there wouldn't drive any value. Instead, the owner would want the store to *feel* so spacious that when customers enter, they feel like it's a special experience, which in turn encourages them to tell their friends, buy more while they're there, and come back more often. Those are what true, owner-driven values look like.

You may not be the owner of your business but you are the owner of your area in the business. So, by focusing on your goals and creating clear, attainable value statements, you will be empowered to take ownership of that effort and drive results within your company. Once these goals and values are defined, you can begin to get into the specifics of execution.

ANALYTICS IN ACTION

While engaged with a major telecommunications company, it became obvious that the customer multiproduct portfolio marketing was becoming overly complex with so many moving parts. Yes, we were able to leverage advanced statistical models to determine each customer's propensity to respond on a given campaign. But combining that information with the customer churn predictor models, cross-referencing with internal red flags (e.g., overdue account bill), overlaying the finance team's customer profitability scores, and even accounting for the complexity of product provisioning possibilities by rooftop/geography was becoming overwhelming.

One by one, we were able to combine each of these facets to build an increasingly improved overall result. For example, when a high propensity to churn on a high-value customer was uncovered, an automatic "product review" was performed, and the customer was notified of the savings being provided to them (churn avoidance). Additionally, while watching the penetration on a marketing campaign, we could monitor when the uptake was over performing, and would immediately accelerate/reallocate marketing spend (ROI maximization).

One surprising early behavioral indicator of predicted movers was uncovered based on reduction in TV minutes viewership and internet usage (quick response opportunity to see if they are interested in any change in services). In the end, these time series and econometric forecasting models combined for incredible results that drove upwards of $1 billion of incremental revenue due to increased response rates and reduced churn.

—Jim Stewart, PhD in management science

CHAPTER 7

ROADMAPPING, PLANNING, AND PRIORITIZATION

A client once told me that the problem with their company's management team was that they were all like minnows in a pond. You drop a piece of bread in, and they all rush right over to that piece and start feeding. But then, the second you drop the next piece in, they all abandon the first piece mid-feast, rush over to the second piece, and begin attacking that one with the same zeal.

Never mind that the first piece was left unfinished. Never mind that they were essentially leaving food on the table (or in this case, in the pond). All that mattered was whatever came next.

I like to call this the *shiny ball syndrome.* In our line of work, the process usually goes something like this: the decision-makers at the company commit to building an analytics program. Unsure of how to get started, they chase down the latest technology or start pursuing the latest buzzword. Thirty, sixty, or ninety days later, a new tech toy has just been released, or a new buzzword has entered the business vernacular. Suddenly, your decision-makers shift away from what they had been doing and start chasing this new shiny ball. Then the same thing happens again sixty days later—and then again sixty days after that.

To succeed with your analytics efforts, you have to protect against shiny ball syndrome. Otherwise, instead of building a cohesive program, you'll just end up with a series of half-baked initiatives that bring no value to your business. In this chapter, we're going to discuss the core tenets of roadmapping, planning, and prioritization that will help you keep your eye on the prize so your analytics program can thrive.

YOU CAN'T EAT THE ELEPHANT IN ONE BITE

A key operating principle to planning is the old axiom that you can't eat the elephant in one bite. You can *try* all you want, but it's impossible. The only way to succeed is to break the effort into smaller, digestible pieces. Remember, you're in it for the long haul, and analytics takes time.

In fact, whatever you're planning to do, it's safe to say that it will likely take three to four times longer to achieve than you expect. For instance, if you expect it will take twenty minutes to mow your lawn, plan for an hour. Sure, mowing the lawn itself may only take twenty minutes, but there are many other tasks associated with the activity—such as moving the garden hose out of the way, having to go get gas for the mower, and maybe even sharpening the mower blade—that will eat into your allotted time.

This isn't just a good rule of thumb for mowing the lawn but also for any business project you might undertake. Say you're putting together a change management/user adoption presentation. The presentation itself is likely to only take a few hours. But just when you're about done, someone says that the VP of Department X should have a chance to chime in before you present the plan to the folks in his division. Then you get word that a new COE (center of excellence) has been put together for change management, so you need to get with them to make sure that nothing being proposed falls outside of their nascent methodology. And *then*, six days before the presentation, it is announced that there is an all-hands meeting the same day of the presentation, and you're told that your presentation, in addition to the all-hands meeting, is too much for one day, so you'll have to scramble to reschedule. Just like that, a three-hour effort has stretched on for days—if not weeks.

Remember, even in the best of conditions, you're going to be combating shiny ball syndrome all throughout this process. No one wants to hear that you're behind. All they want is to know that your work is delivered on time and on budget (and, of course, they also likely want you to include something dear to them that exceeds the agreed-to scope that is driving your timeline and budget). By building in some flextime, you allow yourself the time to get your work done properly without working under any unrealistic expectations. And if by some wonderful stroke of luck nothing unexpected rears up, you are going to look like a genius when you deliver early and under budget.

CRAWL, WALK, RUN

Speaking of geniuses, whenever you're in the early stages of planning an analytics program, there's always going to be a brilliant-sounding question from someone in the room, such as, "What are you doing around predictive modeling with AI? How can we leverage that?"

This question sounds great. However, a warning: without adoption, even the world's most genius idea is worthless. It's negative ROI.

I had to learn this the hard way in my own professional life. Earlier in my career, I always worked to create the best, smartest-sounding presentation that would hopefully wow everyone in the room. But I came to learn that a really well-thought-out idea with little adoption isn't worth much, and much less than just an okay idea that everybody is behind.

Your goal with your analytics program isn't to wow everybody with the most genius, esoteric ideas. It's to change the most people's behavior. Thus, in order to succeed, you must first crawl before you can walk and then walk before you run. Start with the basics and move up in scope and complexity from there.

The crawl-walk-run approach has a couple key benefits. First, it has fewer unknowns up front, which increases your likelihood of success before scaling up your operation. Second, it helps acclimate you to the process. It's much more difficult to run a marathon if you haven't trained ahead of time. Designing and implementing an analytics program is no different.

A good way to think of this is to divide your list of features into *have-to-haves* and *want-to-haves*. In a vacuum, this isn't especially difficult—in fact, it's easy. Your have-to-haves tend to be the low-hanging fruit, the things that will bring the biggest ROI or greatest value capture to your effort and not require moving heaven and earth first. The challenge comes when you get close to crunch time, when, unsurprisingly, people's want-to-haves suddenly become urgent have-to-haves and they argue until they're blue in the face about why a given feature must be included *now*. Don't be surprised when this happens, but remember to keep your eye on the prize; by sticking with your initial have-to-haves, you'll also have a clearer idea of what you'll need down the road.

By keeping your eye on the have-to-haves, you're also keeping your project owners (the folks with P&L responsibility, of course) excited, since achieving these goals will directly map to business results and make them look smart in the process. Further, by focusing on the have-to-haves first, you give yourself a powerful tool in your effort to combat shiny ball syndrome by making your efforts the shiniest ball in the room. After all, sustained and renewed excitement is the best way to drive future success in subsequent cycles.

That said, be careful. Sometimes you may identify an area where you've identified a lot of value, but where the group for whatever reason is notoriously negative. You won't want to ignore this opportunity for too long, but that's probably not the group you want to pick in order to get your analytics program off on the right foot. Otherwise, you'll find it difficult to leverage early success (which will feel nonexistent) into future successes.

PLANNING AND PRIORITIZATION

At this point in the planning process, many companies tend to make the same mistake. After determining their have-to-haves and want-to-haves, they make everything an A priority—everyone wants everything delivered all at once, and no one is willing to wait their turn. Of course, if *everything* is an A priority, then how is *anything* ever going to get done? What do you tackle first?

Organizations that operate in this way have no sense of true prioritization. If nothing can be categorized and documented as an A, B, or C priority, then that means the company culture is unable to prioritize.

Again, sustained analytics is challenging. Most companies aren't able to pull it off (remember, we already know that 80 percent of projects fail). However, you'll make it harder for yourself if your next deadline is eighteen months away. By that time, everyone has all but forgotten about the project.

Besides, a lot can change in eighteen months—sometimes the entire business landscape can transform. When you have regular, and more frequent, deadlines, not only is it easier to stay engaged in the project but it's also more likely that your objectives will remain relevant to your other business needs.

The solution? Follow the steps outlined in this section.

TAKE AN ITERATIVE APPROACH

Because you can't eat the elephant in one bite, it's important that you break up the work into small, manageable pieces and then implement for varying or alternating departments on an iterative and rolling basis. For a two-year analytics project to succeed, for instance, it's essential you take an iterative approach and plan for at least eight cycles, or iterations, in that span.

We suggest quarterly iterations, or ninety-day cycles at a maximum. That way, you're never more than forty-five days away from either an implementation occurring or expecting to occur, which is the perfect amount of time to keep you and your team in the right headspace for success. Plus, anything longer than quarterly and decision-makers or leadership may have already become distracted by the next shiny ball.

Also remember that success breeds success. If you can deliver one piece and then the next, the momentum you begin to build will make everything that much easier.

In all, your iterative process should look something like this:

1. Start with an eighteen- to thirty-six-month roadmap.
2. Within that span, establish quarterly phases.
3. Define the big-picture goals for each phase (e.g., phase one focuses on marketing, phase two focuses on HR, and so on).
4. At the outset of each phase, define the specific goals in value language that will help you meet your big-picture goals.
5. After the completion of about three or four phases (within the first year), revisit your plan and make any necessary adjustments.
6. Continue to extract value to your company via analytics.

When you hold to this cadence, you protect yourself from other stakeholders trying to add in features halfway into the cycle—in other words, making something new an A priority. If this occurs, simply tell that stakeholder that you've already set your priorities for this iteration, but that you'll take their needs into account for the next cycle. Because the iterations are so short, that person is very likely to stay engaged in the process, knowing that their needs are just around the corner from being addressed.

Finally, the last advantage of an iterative approach is that it helps dictate your priorities. After all, there's no way to know for sure what the next step is beyond the one you've just taken until you see your efforts at work in real life. However, almost as soon as your knowledge worker begins using a new analytics solution, they'll begin to see new possibilities that they hadn't previously thought of, and then come back and make a new request for the next iteration.

UTILIZE TIME FENCING

Allocating the appropriate time for each of your own tasks is important, but you also want to set deadlines and delivery expectations for the groups your analytics will support. You want to be able to show that your analytics program actually works and can generate value for your business. The best way to do this is to make your effort time-sensitive by setting—and then sticking to—deadlines. If you say you are going to deliver the first iteration of the program on a given date, you had better deliver it on that date.

We refer to this process as *time fencing*. No matter what you have completed, you must deliver your next iteration by the agreed-to date—it's better to deliver 90 percent of the solution on the time-fenced date than to deliver 110 percent of the solution on a later-than-agreed to date.

In our experience, time fencing is more effective than other approaches, such as scope fencing, because it not only builds accountability but also helps manage expectations. If other team members know that you've roadmapped a series of iterations they won't always demand that their needs be met right away. If their needs are beyond the scope of this iteration, they know that you'll help address their needs in the next go-round.

When you aren't able to manage expectations in this way, everybody and their aunt will be coming to you with requests for different features and capabilities. Since they have no expectation that you'll be delivering more later, they try to selfishly shove all their own needs into the program in the very first cycle. Of course, when you have several people all doing this at once, you're facing too much demand too early, creating huge barriers to success in the process. It would entail you trying to eat the elephant in one bite, which, as we already noted, is a showstopper.

LEVERAGE "DESIGN EDITS"

Pretend that you have a chunk of clay and you're asked to sculpt it into the perfect car. Do you think you'd be able to do it?

Of course not. Sure, you may drive a car, but that doesn't make you a car designer. You wouldn't even know where to start.

Businesses often take this same misguided approach

when first setting out to design their analytics program. They get everyone in the room, set up a clean whiteboard, and say, "All right, tell me what you're looking for."

Just like you're not a car designer, no one in that room is likely to know how to build and design a good analytics program from scratch. If you take this approach to building out your analytics program, you will not see the success that you hope for.

Instead, we recommend what we call the *design edits* approach. In this approach, instead of starting from scratch, we start with a prototype and invite feedback—or edits to the shown design. In other words, we replace the block of clay with a prototype of the car and open the discussion from there. Empowered with a tangible starting point, you're able to offer useful feedback—for instance, the speedometer is too small, the parking brake is in the wrong place, or the radio controls are inconvenient.

It's much easier to edit a prototype than to design a new car from scratch every single time. Knowledge workers aren't in the business of designing analytics. They're in the business of *using* them. By removing the burden of design and instead inviting feedback from a user perspective, you're able to get your program up and running five to ten times faster—and much more efficiently—than if you had started from scratch.

CREATE YOUR TEAMS

In order to make sure the planning and the execution process goes smoothly, it's important that teams and roles are clearly delineated and assigned. We recommend the following team structure.

ANALYTICS PROJECT TEAM (OR CORE TEAM)

The members of this team are the ones assigned to give dedicated time to the project and to actively participate in a daily manner with the project. This is also where the few will represent the many.

This team reports the following to the executive team/steering committee:

- Project roadmap and status (see later in the chapter)
- Goals and concentration areas
- Common lexicon and calculations
- Identified user representatives, and their respective informed proxies, within each phase/concentration area

At the same time, they also work with the governance council to make sure they're using the proper calculations and to resolve any problems with conflicts (see chapter 4).

Managing this communication is the project leader.

This is the person who has the most detailed day-to-day knowledge of the project, how it's progressing, and what the individual team members are working on. The project leader also develops whatever needs to be communicated, working with the steering committee and the governance council to make sure that the team's plans align with the big-picture analytics goals.

EXECUTIVE TEAM/STEERING COMMITTEE

Managing this team is the executive sponsor, or project owner, the person with P&L responsibility in charge of ensuring that the project is on track to meet its carefully defined goals—and that those goals are tied to hard value (see chapter 3). The project owner will lean heavily on the project leader for assistance with status updates, document prep, coordinating logistics, etc.

To understand the importance of this committee with its executive sponsor, let's use an analogy. Imagine that your project team is your dentist, and you as the executive sponsor are the patient. Your dentist is really excited about keeping your teeth healthy. They want you to brush three times a day, to floss twice a day, gargle for thirty seconds, and to chew every bite of food at least thirty times. Everywhere they look, they see opportunity, and they're ready to go all-in on your mouth.

All these recommendations sound great, but your job is to pump the brakes a little bit. You want to have a healthy mouth, but you're pretty sure your dentist is going a little overboard. From their list of recommendations, you're going to choose the ones that go the furthest in achieving your goals—and therefore bringing value to your business.

GOVERNANCE COUNCIL

This group works across projects, providing big-picture guidance on key parameters and definitions that keep everyone on the same page. In the case of disagreement of definitions/calculations of related terms across project teams, the governance council is the tiebreaker. For example, if you have time zone considerations for online orders—in other words, if there is disagreement on when to define the day as being over—then the council would act as a tiebreaker. Similarly, if you're unsure whether to define sell through as EOP versus BOP, again the governance council could act as tiebreaker.

If an enterprise governance council doesn't exist, it's not the end of the world. Just have your core team act as the first, de facto, governance council for cross-departmental nomenclature and calculation definitions.

EXECUTING YOUR PLANS

Now that you've established priorities and created your teams, it's time to execute. The following considerations will go a long way in helping you to keep your program on schedule and on target.

BE ACCOUNTABLE

No matter how hard you've worked on setting priorities and establishing a decision-making structure through your working teams, the time will come when someone comes to you—be it a department member with non-direct representation on the core team, a departmental executive, or the VP—and they're going to ask you to throw in a new feature, which they consider absolutely essential. Luckily, you've been warned about this exact outcome all throughout this chapter, so when this moment comes, you'll know exactly what to do.

First, since you're following an iterative approach, you'll ask whether this request can wait until the next phase, where you'll have more capability to implement it properly. Second, sometimes a request has a clear strategic purpose or if the stakeholder is unwilling to roll their newfound needs into the next cycle, bring a formal request to the project team/steering committee, who will make one of two choices:

1. Stick with the existing plan and make a special note to focus on this requested need in the next phase.
2. Delay the project to include the new need. An official decision from the steering committee is important.

Whatever the case, don't make the decision alone. The worst thing to do would be to pick one path or the other without the overall team being part of the decision itself, as that would be a surefire way to guarantee a full volley of arrows in your back.

If you're going to face delays, you still need to hold yourself and your team accountable. Clearly communicating the change of plans, setting the expectation, and getting everyone on the same page is the best way to do that. If something is due on March 31, then it's due on March 31. If for any reason a request comes along that causes you to miss that date, then it's imperative that you be accountable and eliminate all ambiguity from what that delay will mean via proper documentation and communication.

ESTABLISH DEDICATED IMPLEMENTATION RESOURCES

In chapter 3, we talked about the difference between tactical and strategic roles within a business. As a refresher, while those occupying a strategic role have a greater long-term impact on a business, those in tactical roles are essential for short-term stability. Equally essential is that you understand the difference between these two types of workers, and that you define and dedicate roles accordingly.

To make this work, there are two important steps you must take.

Step 1: Define the Level of Dedication

Whoever is on your core team, determine how much time they're going to spend on the project on a weekly basis. For instance, you could decide the team will spend four hours on this project for the next twelve weeks, with a full sixteen hours dedicated to the first two weeks. With their responsibilities clearly time-bound, those workers should have a good idea of what work they're going to have to off-load in order to free up their time.

Step 2: Designate Informed Proxies

Sick days, vacations, and family emergencies all happen. However, just because a person is on vacation doesn't mean the work should grind to a halt, causing the project to push out. In these scenarios, it's okay to ask a coworker to step in and help out. That said, it's unacceptable to pick a random coworker out of the hallway and ask them to sit in on a meeting without debriefing them ahead of time. That accomplishes nothing and wastes everyone's time.

Instead, designate informed proxies—employees who have been briefed on the program, kept up to speed by the representative on the core team that they are the proxy for, and empowered to act on behalf of that representative. These informed proxies can help with the decision-making process and ensure everything moves forward. Just remember that for this approach to be effective, education and communication are key. Be proactive and make sure the proxy is constantly kept up to speed well, as getting sick or having an out-of-office emergency isn't predictable or planned ahead of time.

ALIGN INCENTIVES WITH YOUR OBJECTIVES

We once worked with a luxury retailer who defined their most important customers as anyone who spent more than $5,000 a year on their products. Those people, they decided, would get the premium treatment. Anyone who didn't meet this threshold effectively didn't exist. It wasn't that these lower spenders weren't important. However, whenever a line is drawn with any definition, people tend to treat those above and below that line as a major demarcation in their beliefs, and their behavior follows that belief.

Our analysts quickly realized this was an opportunity. We

determined that this retailer had a huge swath of customers who regularly spent less than $5,000 a year—but who had a 97 percent likelihood of spending that amount or more per year within the next five years based on where they were in the customer life cycle and assuming they continue to be treated correctly. Sure, these customers weren't big spenders *yet*, but if the retailer continued to ignore them, they likely never would be.

With the available data, we were able to identify which sales associates these up-and-comers usually shopped with. Then we gave those associates a list of these up-and-comer customers and instructed the associates to treat them as if they were already high-value customers.

At first, the associates balked at the idea. "Oh, I know this shopper," they would say. "She doesn't spend enough." Since they were paid on commission, the associates didn't care that the analytics said these customers might become big spenders in the future; they had no incentive to help them in the present.

It was clear that the way the sales associates were incentivized did not align with the retailer's newly identified objectives. Situations like this are all too common. In many ways, for instance, this situation was similar to the problem Telco had encountered in chapter 2. While the company didn't want installation orders lasting more than seven days, employees weren't incentivized to honor the spirit of that request and so chose to game the system instead.

Luckily for the luxury retailer, closing the incentive/objective gap wasn't especially difficult. All we had to do was add a bonus spiff around any incremental sales the associates were able to produce while working with the up-and-comers. That way, it became worth the associates' time to give these future big spenders their time and attention.

LET YOUR VALUES PLAY TIEBREAKER

Up to this point in the planning process, you've defined your goals and values; you've created a time-fenced, iterative schedule; and you have a team of the few representing the many who is leveraging design edits to finalize requirements and hand off the program to the implementation team. Right around this point, something frustrating—but entirely predictable—is likely to happen. Out of left field, a higher-up exec pops into the room and says, "I need to have this metric, or the project isn't worth doing at all."

Be prepared for this moment. It's not a matter of *if,* but *when.*

This is why it's so important to carefully define your goals and values at the outset. That way, when the exec pops in and makes their request, you and the core team are already prepared to view that request in terms of value added. How does the exec's request enhance the business? Will it add two basis points to revenue? Will it reduce expenses by 2 percent? In either case, how does that value compare with your currently established value statements?

Running the exec's request through your value-added filter will help clear up the picture quickly and give you a sense of prioritization. By that point, you should know whether the request is important enough to delay rollout by four weeks at a cost of $150,000 or not. Whatever the case, here is your executive sponsor's opportunity to shine. After reviewing the request and filtering it through both a P&L lens and your team's value statements, the executive sponsor and steering committee will either give the thumbs up to the eleventh-hour request or say, "We're going with what we already have, but we'll address your request in the next phase."

This is one of the beauties of iteration: it doesn't have to be one and done. Your project leader never has to say no to one of their bosses. Instead, they get to say, "Yes, we are on it and plan a rollout to test within the next three months (which happens to be the next phase)," which is a much easier pill to swallow.

ANALYTICS IN ACTION

Vince had been founded as a wholesale brand (meant to be distributed in major department stores and top specialty stores in the US and abroad). Vince-branded stores were meant to provide marketing exposure in key flagship cities rather than as the primary revenue channel.

However, after ten successful years, this started to shift with both the increased penetration of e-commerce along with the strategic decision by prior management to aggressively open Vince-branded stores throughout the US. By 2017, it was apparent that the brand had become overdistributed and exposed by the organic growth of e-commerce (inclusive of Vince.com; the department stores' websites, and also the pure play global sites that had become so relevant, including Net-a-Porter, Mytheresa, and Farfetch, just to name a few). Adding to the saturation was the full transparency that alerted the customer when it was on sale at virtually any location (thus having the effect that if it were on sale somewhere, it was on sale everywhere), which dramatically lowered profit margins.

Looking at the trend of the business and projecting that forward, the data showed that this was going to continue to pressure the financials. We looked at the three main channels of distribution to determine whether we could scale back to alleviate the competitive pressures we had caused. Our own brick-and-mortar stores weren't a real option, as most of the leases were new and therefore we had little opportunity to close the stores. Scaling back e-commerce was not an option based on its organic growth and need to best service the changing needs and shopping patterns of the consumer. That left the wholesale channel as the only option.

Turning again to the data, we ran different scenarios on what we would need to have happen if we took supply out of the marketplace in order to replace the lost volume with more profitable and sustainable business elsewhere. In the end, we made the difficult decision to exit two of our largest partners (Saks and Bloomingdales) with the strategy to funnel the lost business into the other channels and stores and to do so in a more profitable way both from sell-throughs and infrastructure needed to support the business.

—Brendan Hoffman, CEO, Vince

GET READY TO DIG IN

Now that you have that final hurdle sorted out, you're ready to move on to part 3 of the book and begin implementing your analytics program. Before you read on, however, a reminder: if you want to succeed, you're going to have to approach analytics differently than you have approached other transactional projects. That means following the steps outlined here in part 2 and staying on target.

The definition of insanity is doing the same thing and expecting different results. We all know that, yet often when we have this exact same conversation with our clients, the information goes in one ear and out the other. They nod their heads, say "Yes, absolutely," and then they're great for about three weeks.

Afterward, they're right back to their old patterns. The supposedly dedicated employees are being pulled off the project to go fight fires in the company, unprepped proxies are being sent to meetings without a clue of how they can contribute (and unwilling to make decisions), and others are blowing off the work entirely. It's a tragic sight to behold, but also an entirely avoidable one.

Carrying your efforts through the implementation phase means living up to the promise of all your careful planning, goals, and value statements. This is no small challenge—which, if you've ever tried to get fit or otherwise improve yourself in some way, you might relate. For instance, imagine that you just read a self-help book that you really connected with. It made you feel more powerful and motivated than you have in a long time, and immediately you started down the path that book set you on in hopes of becoming a better person.

A week later, you're off the path.

You pick up another self-help book, and the same thing happens: you get excited, start down the path, and then lose interest and quit.

A month later, the same thing happens again.

After three months and several false starts, you're no closer to creating a better you than you were after you picked up that first book. You *want* to improve yourself, and you're certainly putting in plenty of effort, but you haven't been able to maintain your focus and sustain your interest.

This cycle of false starts and dashed hopes doesn't just apply to the world of self-help. Think of the gym sign-ups early January each year, and, yes it happens all the time in business—and especially in analytics—as well. The path forward isn't especially complicated, but being persistent with your approach and putting consistent work in can be challenging.

But while none of this is easy, it *is* worth it. If you can sustain the effort to keep your analytics program running, then you will have "created a moat around your business," as I like to say, separating yourself from the 80 percent of businesses that made the attempt at analytics adoption, but couldn't keep their eye on the ball long enough to see the rewards.

PART 3

TURNING DATA INTO INFORMATION

CHAPTER 8

SOURCING AND STORING YOUR DATA

One of our clients enlisted us to help analyze the data from their customer base, which they said was about 90,000 people. However, when they sourced all their data with us, we found the number to be much higher—a full 112,000 entries.

This wasn't a small discrepancy. It was a huge error, and our client couldn't account for it at first. Working line item by line item, we began to see the problem: the data had been entered fairly consistently, but the process of pulling that data from the source system created formatting errors. Specifically, some of the customer data had been inserted using carriage returns—which created multiple entries out of the same customer, or "phantom records"—

while others hadn't. There were no bad actors here and no one was especially at fault, but the data sourcing process had created unexpected formatting errors.

We found other problems as well. Some of the entries came with small notes that weren't part of the data set: "Customer Location #12. Ask for Kathy. She's the nice one at the front desk." With all due respect to Kathy and her nice demeanor, that note was irrelevant to the core data and was hindering our ability to create useful information out of the data set.

Another time, we were working with an online dating service that was interested in sponsoring and promoting local meet-ups for their users. At the time, this service was underwritten by a large tobacco company, so they were holding one event in particular that was geared toward smokers at a popular local bar.

To help market this event, the dating service enlisted us to work through their database of 23,000 local smokers and identify who might be interested in attending. But when we started working with the data, something seemed off. Were there *really* 23,000 smokers within five miles of this event? That number sounded unrealistically high.

It was.

The total number of members in the entire area—smoker or not—was only 8,000, a full 15,000 people *less* than the supposed smoking members in the area.

Something funny had happened with the data. After a deep dive, we identified the problem. Whenever we went to identify the smokers in the area, some members were showing up in the results two or three times, or even more. Why? Because they had checked multiple different smoking boxes when filling out their profile—one for "smoker," one for "occasional smoker," one for "social smoker," and one for "chain smoker." If those same people had also checked off "smoker," "social smoker," etc., when defining their ideal partner, it only multiplied the effect.

Because the data wasn't being extracted correctly—any member who had checked off more than one box was being counted as more than one person. Again, the problem was no one's fault; it was just a result of the nuances of how certain queries talk to the computer's database. It was an easy issue to spot once we looked for it, but the whole point of analytics is that you shouldn't *have* to look for it.

Analytics is the process of sourcing data, turning that data into information, using that information to generate insights, and then implementing those insights to monetize your data. For this process to go right, it's essential that you approach your data capture with tremendous care. Otherwise, even the smallest error can cause things to get messy fast. Garbage in, garbage out.

In this chapter, we'll outline the best practices for sourcing, storing, and exporting your data. As we move through these practices, remember, your data serves as the basis of everything else you're building in your program. If you're working with faulty data from the outset, then you lose all your future insights. For that reason, it's essential that you clearly define procedures to ensure that the data you source is both accurate and properly recorded.

WHAT TYPES OF DATA SHOULD BE SOURCED?

It's a big world out there, with untold amounts of data available to be sourced, sorted, and eventually converted into useful information for your business. But here's the problem: With so many possible avenues to explore and so much potential data to capture, how do you decide what data to source and what data to ignore?

There's no single answer for this. In fact, as your needs and goals change, so too might your sourcing priorities. In other words, you will want to ask the question of what data to source constantly. The following questions will help guide your decision-making process:

- What value (refer to your defined goals) are you trying to capture?
- What actions must you take to capture that value?
- What insights are needed for that action to occur?

To give an example of why questions like these are so important, imagine that you work for the HR department at your company. For various reasons, it's important that you hold onto employee data after they quit rather than delete them from your system. At the same time, other duties require you to run various analytics pertaining to employee performance so you can determine, for instance, who might be a rising star within the company.

There is potential for a problem here. If you're not careful in how you source your data—or in this case *what* you source—you run the risk of including former employees or employees who have given notice ahead of your rising star reports. After all, people are coming and leaving every day. If you don't update your analytics viewpoint accordingly, you could end up with a dramatically inflated sense of the number of rising stars within the company.

In this example, imagine one of your questions at the outset of the program was, "Do we source data on who currently works for the company, who has given notice, and who has departed?" Your answer is unequivocally *yes*.

This data helps you capture value, generate important insights, and take appropriate action.

If you don't focus your data sourcing efforts in this way, you run the risk of what we call *scope creep:* the more data you source, the more data you *want* to source—whether that data is valuable to you or not.

This might sound harmless, but it's a surefire way to fall behind schedule and lose track of your priorities. The businesses that keep tumbling down rabbit holes end up expanding scope without adding any value to the conversation. It's easy to want to go and source that next data set, but if you don't need it or can't actionate it, you're only wasting your time.

Let's dive a little deeper to see how this plays out. The following examples, drawn from our experiences with actual businesses, illustrate the business's starting point (their stated project goal as a value statement), their likely data needs, and the kinds of scope creep that inevitably set in.

EXAMPLE #1

Value statement: "To reduce 80 percent of the financial analysts' time spent assembling data."

LIKELY INITIAL DATA NEEDS	LIKELY SCOPE CREEP IN THE FIRST ITERATION
• Last week's sales • Product allocated costs and margin estimates • Key attributes—financial reporting calendar, customer-region-company rollups, etc.	• Accounts receivables aging • Sales rep tenure demographics • Cost coefficients of various product transportation methods

EXAMPLE #2

Value statement: "To be able to accurately identify and track 'rising star' employees. To implement reporting that ensures the rising stars are meaningfully engaged by management every sixty days."

LIKELY INITIAL DATA NEEDS	LIKELY SCOPE CREEP IN THE FIRST ITERATION
• Segmented active employees list • Management contact/ engagement activities • Employee start date, promotion activity	• Frequency of employee logins to the VPN • Employee educational background • Drive time from employee home to office

EXAMPLE #3

Value statement: "To improve email campaigns by 10 percent without sweetening the offers."

LIKELY INITIAL DATA NEEDS	LIKELY SCOPE CREEP IN THE FIRST ITERATION
• Active customers list • Outbound contact by offer, channel, and cadence • Customer activity (e.g., inbound inquiries, web clicks, sales)	• Competitive activity • Weather • Social media mentions

In your own analytics efforts, you will no doubt see how your own curiosity can get the best of you and tempt you to start tumbling down new rabbit holes. Whenever you find that scope creep, well, *creeping* in, just remember these words: ask not what data you can get, but what value you can create for your business.

WHERE DO YOU FIND YOUR DATA?

Most companies want to know what their competitors are doing. This is a natural impulse, but it often comes at the cost of knowing what *they* are doing. Businesses generate tons of internal data every day, and yet most of it goes overlooked, unnoticed, or forgotten. It's almost as if it's *verboten*, like you're not supposed to even understand it, much less use it.

We recommend taking the opposite approach: internal data first, external data second (and only after you have captured all the low-hanging fruit from your own data).

Some businesses don't bother with their internal data because they assume they already know everything that's going on inside their business. This is untrue 100 percent of the time. The truth is, you're never going to know what you don't know unless you measure and analyze it.

Once you do this, you'll see that focusing on internal data

has considerable benefits. It's easier to get to, for one thing, but it's also richer. With competitors' data, you usually only see the tip of the iceberg. Imagine you're a retail company interested in what your fellow retailers are doing. Do you really think you're going to learn all you need to know about their operation by sending secret shoppers in to take pictures, look at the inventory on the shelves, and make price comparisons? Sure, you might get *some* value out of that, but you're not getting the full picture.

With such an incomplete picture, that data will be difficult to understand. In truth, understanding your own data is challenging enough. The difference, however, is that you will get more value from the effort with your own data than you would if you spent all your time poring over your competitors' data.

YOU DON'T NEED TO SOURCE EVERYTHING

Normally when you're trying to predict something in the future, two or three metrics will give you the great majority of the data necessary to make accurate predictions. While you can refine your efforts somewhat by sourcing data on five, six, or even seven metrics, the incremental value of each additional attribute/metric diminishes exponentially in a phenomenon known as "the law of diminishing returns." In fact, if you push too far, you're likely to run up a negative ROI.

This goes against our instincts. It's easy to get caught up in the idea that more equals better. (Have you ever asked yourself if you *really* need five blades on your razor?) Often, however, that's simply not the case.

A good rule of thumb here is to follow the Pareto Principle, more commonly referred to as "the 80/20 rule": 20 percent of the data attributes are going to give you 80 percent of the information you need. Focus on the metrics that add the most value first. Then, if you still need a more complete picture, feel free to add another metric or two into the mix. If you don't think it's going to help, don't spend the effort.

HOW TO SOURCE AND STORE YOUR DATA THE RIGHT WAY

A lot can go wrong when you're sourcing and storing your data. A simple error in how you input and sort your information can have a massive negative impact on your ability to create accurate insights that are useful to your business. Similarly, it can also slow down the responsiveness of your analytics solution and cause people to lose their "stream of consciousness" analysis and ultimately abandon a solution.

It's no surprise, then, that most analytics efforts suffer serious setbacks during this phase. When you don't know what sorts of errors to look for and steer clear of, it's easy to screw things up. By implementing the following guidelines, you will have a guaranteed approach for getting your analytics efforts off on the right foot.

CAPTURE DATA AS CLOSE AS POSSIBLE TO THE ORIGINAL SOURCE SYSTEM

The original transaction system holds the truth. Because of this, many times people want to report directly against it. We recommend that you capture your data as close to the original transaction system as possible, but *not* on the system itself. There are two reasons for this:

1. You could create a conflict that messes up the transaction system.
2. Analytics information isn't the same as the transactional data in the system.

In an earlier example, we talked about a company that wanted access to all of its past twelve months of customer usage summed up and stack ranked. Had we summed that usage data in the original transaction system, we would have had no way of contextualizing the customers who had been with the company for less than a year. Three months in the system would be three months in the system, and we would have had no way to work with that data.

Instead, we extracted it and stored it in our analytics system (sometimes referred to as a *data mart* or *data warehouse*). That way, we could go to that three-month data point, modeled and filled in what the other nine months of data likely would have looked like, and produced a true projected year of use for the new customer.

Depending on the original transaction system, we may have been able to go into it and produce some fake data to generate the same result. This would have only created a problem, however, the next time someone else accessed the system to determine how much actual usage there had been over the previous year. Because we would have altered the data, that person would have produced an incorrect number. While it is possible to work in the original transaction system, doing so is not only dangerous but also limited.

GET GRANULAR

Since you're wary of scope creep, you're committed to not collecting every single possible piece of data. For the data that you *do* extract, however, work to keep it as granular as possible. Now is not the time to roll it up and summarize it (that part comes in chapter 9). If you do, you run a very good risk of losing data. Store your data at the most atomic level possible and then make a copy so that you don't lose anything in case the system goes down.

One of our clients had a habit of rolling many of its customers into one entity, even if doing so only created problems rather than solved them. For instance, they serviced a large number of different McDonald's, each of which, as a franchisee, had different owners. Each should have received their own separate entry, and because of how their algorithm was set up, all McDonald's were rolled into a single entity.

Another of our clients had a similar issue when setting up their algorithm. One of their clients was a large corporation called EDS, so they used the term "EDS" to sort through and create a single entity for their data sourcing efforts. The problem was they also served a client called Ed's Garage—which, because it was entered as "Eds Garage" without the apostrophe, got lumped in with EDS.

Skilled analysts are able to identify and pull out these issues, but your analytics effort will run much more smoothly if they never have to. For this reason, we recommend that you collect and store your data as granularly as possible. That way, if an issue like this arises, your analytics team can unwind the error and reprocess the data back out how it should be.

If you're worried about the logistics of storing all that data, there's no need to be. Data is cheap to store—and only getting cheaper. Advancements in storage capabilities move fast. Just to give you an idea:

- Any smartphone has more power in it than all the computer systems that combined to put a man on the moon.[7]
- The three terabyte external back-up drive sitting on top of my desk can store more information than all of the combined data in the world that was stored online in 1997.[8]
- Between 2017 and 2019 alone, 90 percent of the data existing in the world was generated.

It's true that the more data you store, the more costs you're likely to incur. However, even with large storage needs, the cost is nothing compared to the value of the insights you might gain from it. If you're spending $10 a month to store data that leads to $10,000 worth of insights, isn't that cost worth it?

ALIGN THE OUTPUT WITH THE INPUT

As we saw in the opening story to this chapter, you don't want your data misrepresenting how many records you

---

7.   Michio Kaku. "Your cell phone has more computing power than NASA circa 1969." Knopf Doubleday Publishing Group. http://knopfdoubleday.com/2011/03/14/your-cell-phone/.

8.   Michael Lesk. "How Much Information Is There in the World?" http://www.lesk.com/mlesk/ksg97/ksg.html.

actually have. Make sure that the number of records that come out are the exact number of records that you *expect* to come out. We call this automated process "data health checks." If you're looking for eighty-eight thousand customers and your system produces 112,000, then you've got an error somewhere.

PRACTICE SELF-HEALING

In analytics terms, self-healing is a way of tracking and reconciling all the data you've sourced from day to day. At a minimum, it's important to keep records of your daily outputs for at least the past seven to twenty-one days. That way, if new data pops up where it's not supposed to, or if you missed a specific data set on a certain day, you'll be able to identify it and determine why.

Practicing self-healing can help in a big way. For instance, imagine that you're sourcing financial or accounting data. Tomorrow you may receive a check that was dated for today. Naturally, that check won't show up in your feed today, since you haven't received it yet. However, when you receive it tomorrow, because it's dated for a different day, it could slip through the system on a daily-only feed—similarly with backdated transactions. Self-healing allows you to go back in time, check through your records over a given time period, and account for these small discrepancies.

ANALYTICS IN ACTION

Working with PDX Inc., a provider of pharmacy software and healthcare solutions to over ten thousand pharmacies, we determined from the underlying data that there was a huge monetizable analytic opportunity in providing each customer, down to the individual pharmacy level, access to valuable patient-level prescription and healthcare data, and thus ultimately providing each pharmacy customer with a better picture of the patients they serve. This in turn would ensure the pharmacy remained competitive and also compliant with industry needs and standards.

Building and supporting the infrastructure necessary to maintain strict HIPAA standards in data security meant an enormous on-site hardware investment that didn't make financial sense. However, the inexpensive nature of storing data in the cloud opened up the possibility of leveraging a data warehouse in the cloud too, and Snowflake Computing filled that need. Despite the volume of data from billions of individual prescription fills, the service-level agreements (SLAs), security required for the individual users across thousands of locations, and the unique users' customized query needs, an affordable SaaS solution was developed.

By spinning up multiple compute clusters every morning and then mothballing them each night to reduce computing costs, leveraging the elastic environment to flex-scale only when necessary to accommodate the growing needs of the pharmacies, the Explore Dx Platform has created a new revenue stream for PDX and allowed the pharmacies to easily identify their highest-performing technicians with the lowest error rates to help improve utilization rates and to quickly uncover prescriptions that insurance companies inadequately reimbursed. Better access to that atomic-level data has improved data-driven decision-making, thus improving patient outcomes.

—Todd Crosslin, VP, healthcare strategy, Snowflake Computing

—Dan Murphy, regional director of sales (TOLA & LATAM), Snowflake Computing

CREATE REAL CONNECTIONS

If your data is ever connected, you need to make sure it's a *real* connection and that it's not too loose. To give an example of what we mean, consider what happens when you source phone numbers and throw them together with other client data. This sounds like a good idea, but phone numbers get changed all the time. I personally still receive phone calls asking for a woman named Molly, who apparently isn't great at paying her bills. Molly hasn't had the number I now use for years, and yet that loose connection between the number and the person continues to create problems for me (and I assume her bill collectors).

Think twice when considering whether to link data such as phone numbers or addresses and then believing that link is gospel. Numbers change all the time, just like people move all the time. Unless you're careful with how you go about it, these kinds of connections aren't the truth on their own.

TAKE YOUR TIME

Sourcing and storing your data isn't sexy. It's detailed, painstaking work. Done correctly, and you'll be well set up to generate valuable insight after valuable insight down the road. Done incorrectly, and you're likely to encounter all sorts of problems downstream—inaccurate, unreliable data being one of them. Again: garbage in, garbage out.

By following these steps, you can be certain that you're going through the right systems, sourcing data accurately, and storing them at the appropriate level so that, no matter what your future needs, you will be able to go back and access them.

To be clear, this isn't a matter of *if*, but a matter of *when*. After all, it's almost impossible to know the difference between what you *think* you want versus what you *actually* want when you first set up your analytics program. Just look at your Netflix or DVR queue if you don't believe me. How many of those programs have sat there for weeks, months, or even years because you *thought* you'd want to watch them, even though you never have?

It's no different with analytics. But the good news is that if you give this step in the process the attention and care it deserves, you'll be well positioned to access whatever data you may need and begin assembling that data into useful information.

CHAPTER 9

TRANSFORMING DATA INTO INFORMATION

Let's say you love football. You want to know everything about your favorite team, how they did last week, how they're preparing for next week, and any big trades that might be coming down the pipeline. Right now, you're especially interested in how your team might design its game plan around a particularly challenging opponent, specifically what plays they're going to run and how that might work out for them.

If you wanted to learn more, you could head over to the NFL website, download every single play your team has run from the line of scrimmage for the entire season, and start to build a picture of what their playbook might look like next week. You could get as granular as you wanted, learning how much time was left, whether it was a running or passing play, what the outcome was, and so on.

Within those tens of thousands of lines of data, all the information you ever wanted lies buried. But the sheer volume is overwhelming. It's too much for you to do anything productive with. Staring at reams of data in page-down after page-down views, amplified with scrolling for days across columns, isn't going to make the light bulb go off.

Besides, you already have a much better alternative available to you: head over to ESPN.com. There, instead of looking at raw data, you're looking at carefully sorted information. All the highlights, trends, and play history are right there at your fingertips. Even better, the website is designed to create a seamless user experience. It's colorful, full of images, and easy to use. Not only is the site informative, it's fun.

Now, imagine you're at work and you want to figure out the answer to a pressing business question. Here, you only have one option: pull out the appropriate Excel spreadsheet and sift through the seemingly infinite rows of data—just like you would have if you had downloaded every play from the NFL's website. After staring at the spreadsheet for a while, just like you've done so many times before, you'll be able to sort everything out and pull out the information, but it's going to take a while—and you're going to have to repeat this process every single time you want more information.

There's got to be a better way, you think to yourself.

There is.

Your data at work can be as easy to use, access, and understand as using the internet. You shouldn't have to pore through lines of data trying to find the answer to a pressing question. Instead, you should let a computer do what a computer *should* do. Assigning humans this task is inefficient, a waste of time and labor, and unfulfilling. It just doesn't make sense from a business perspective—again, no knowledge worker's job description says "fool around with data."

If you have sourced and stored your data properly, you will be able to answer any question you might have almost instantaneously. Just like ESPN.com can almost instantly tell you how Tom Brady has performed the last ten games, what his completion percentages are against next week's opponent, or any other piece of information you can think of, your analytics system should be able to deliver the same depth of information at the same speed and with the same level of accuracy.

In this chapter, you will learn how to turn your data into useful information. At this point in the analytics process, you will start to learn valuable clues as to how your business is performing. From there, as we will see in later chapters, you will have everything you need to generate and monetize valuable insights for your business.

IT'S ALL ABOUT DATA QUALITY

Imagine you're trying to hire a new regional salesperson. This process will likely play out along one of the following scenarios:

- **You have good information.** You know exactly what sales you're missing and what customer growth you're not capturing, and from that information you can decide whether to hire your candidate.
- **You have bad information.** You don't know you have bad information, so you think it's true. From that information, you decide whether or not to hire a person—putting you in a situation that could be worse than having no information at all.
- **You have no information.** In this case, you could ask a few questions, look around, and make a decision based on what you've learned.

As these scenarios show, having bad information is worse than having no information whatsoever. The question then becomes, how do you make sure you don't have bad information?

With your core team structure (see chapter 7), let the few represent the many. Your team should be able to decide what information should be included, what won't, and what the quality should be. Additionally, they should also make decisions on how to define certain terms— like the difference between a new customer and an active customer.

To give another example, imagine again that you own a retail company. A customer visits your website and orders something. While it's one thing to count the total number of orders on the day, it's another to separate your customers into different categories, such as how many active customers you have versus your total number of customers.

The idea is plain enough, but consider how you might approach this question. For instance, would you separate these customers out by address? That could work, but if three different people live at that house—all of whom order from your business (like at a sorority or frat house)— then you won't get very reliable results. Perhaps you could group those three people into a single household instead, which is a somewhat different concept, but again, some-one would have to decide that.

There are challenges inherent in identifying your customer's *period*, let alone sorting them into *new*, *active*, and *dormant* categories. It may be easy to say that a customer who buys from you every week is an active customer, but when do they become dormant? After five weeks? Ten? Seventeen? What is the exact point when they're no longer active? This is a particularly challenging definition for you as a retail shop owner, as your customers go away with a whimper, quiet and slowly, whereas the customers of a bank, for example, go away with a bang—they close out their accounts.

Questions like these will go unanswered unless you have a designated person—or team of people—to answer them for you. To make sure that all your knowledge workers have the quality and depth of data that they require in order to do their jobs, let the few represent the many. Let one person on your team take a first cut at defining the parameters, and then let the rest of the team work together to finalize those definitions.

Again, this human component is what makes analytics projects so challenging. Most technology projects are transactional; you pick a tech or software solution, your team implements it, and you're off to the races. With analytics, however, every question comes with a degree of ambiguity, which is why having a team of skilled decision-makers is so important to success. This creates tremendous opportunity, both for success and failure. How you define the parameters, right or wrong, will affect everything you do downstream.

To solve for the human element, your core team must be laser focused on setting expectations and standardizing terms. For instance, one time one of our clients wanted to solve their problem with back orders. One of the executives had noticed that they had run up $110,000 worth of back orders, and they wanted to solve the problem. Another employee said many of the supposed back orders were already on a truck and en route, so it was really only about a $72,000 problem. Still another employee had a different number for the value of back orders, and so on.

After hearing this conversation unfold, we could see that the real problem wasn't the back orders, but the ambiguity surrounding them. Whether the value of back orders was $110,000 or $72,000 didn't matter. The problem that no one could settle on a fixed number *did* matter. Everyone was taking their own one-off approach to defining the issue. With multiple different numbers, despite all showing there was a problem, no action was being taken. But until everyone got on the same page with how they defined terms and sourced and transformed the data, no amount of analytics could help them sort the issues.

Without standardization, your analytics effort can't be

action driven. When eleven people are all analyzing the same problem but in different ways, no action is taken except to go back and reanalyze the data to see why everyone is coming up with different numbers. That's all expense with no value and no ROI.

When creating your working definitions, remember: good enough is better than perfect. In fact, good enough actually *is* perfect for directional understanding. Each team member could have a different argument for why their definition is the best, but those arguments aren't going to move the business forward. If you wait for the perfect definition, you will never move from sourcing to action. Create your definition, implement it, and revise as needed with the next iteration of the program. As long as you've been going granular with your data sourcing (see chapter 8), then any changes in definition will have zero impact on the data itself. It can't—as data is facts and facts never change. What changes is the transformation, and thus the information derived from the data.

STRUCTURE AND SUMMARIZE FOR A QUICK RESPONSE

Say you run a commercial airline. You offer a good variety of flights and competitive prices, but your website doesn't work very well. Travelers input their information—the departure and arrival dates, the number of passengers, the amount of luggage, etc.—and then wait a full five minutes for the system to return results. This is a dramatically unacceptable amount of time to wait, so it's no surprise, then, that a huge number of prospective customers end up abandoning their efforts and booking with another airline.

If your customers won't accept such outlandish wait times, neither will your knowledge workers. To get to actionable decision-making, your knowledge workers must be able to easily access and use relevant information in a seamless and timely manner. That's why it's essential that your data is structured and summarized in a way that enables a quick response. When we mean quick, we mean near-instantaneous. Large, data-heavy searches might result in a ten to fifteen-second wait (and this should only be for use by power users and data scientists), but standard searches for the knowledge workers should have little to no lag.

This may go against the more common impulse, which is to dump all the data you can on someone and say, "Here, just have that. Ask any questions you want." If you assemble your information in this way, you're not going to have a good response time. Just like ESPN.com does with its NFL page, your data must be structured in a way that reflects how it's going to be used. It needs to be structured and summarized so that every time your knowledge workers ask a question they receive a quick and accurate response.

This may sound simple—it may even sound like a no-brainer—but we've found this is one of the most challenging parts of the whole analytics process. We humans can be difficult. We can get so caught up in the data available to us that we tend to lose sight of what our goals are, or what's relevant or helpful.

DEMOCRATIZE YOUR DATA

Some companies like to overprotect their data. Everything they source is effectively hidden behind a web of passwords, authorizations, and permissions hurdles, making it difficult for knowledge workers to access that information and drive action for the business. With every access request, the paranoia sets in: "Why do you need it? Who's going to have it? What are you going to do with it?" They protect their information as if it's somehow a limited asset.

The truth is, the more people that use your information, the more valuable it is.

We don't advocate for a completely open data policy. If a worker doesn't need access to certain information, they don't need to see it (especially as it pertains to HR data, for example). However, for everybody who *does* need to see it, that information should be easily open and available without forcing them to jump through a million hoops every time they want to access it.

YOU AREN'T MANAGING WHAT YOU AREN'T MEASURING

Management guru Peter Drucker famously said, "What gets measured gets managed."

This statement lies at the heart of analytics adoption. If you can *know* whether you've met your goals, then why waste your time guessing? How can you quantify progress toward your goal if you aren't measuring it?

Imagine that you work in HR, and you're working on improving the interaction between a couple employees who lately have been at odds with each other. In the simplest terms possible, your goal is to get those employees to be nicer to each other. The question is, in the weeks that follow, how do you know whether they have or not?

To answer that question, you could follow two basic approaches:

- **The honor system.** The employees are told to be kinder and more respectful. Every week, you ask them whether they are. Most likely, whether it's true or not, they're going to reply in the affirmative. At worst, they'll probably say, "I don't know." In any case, you'll have to take their word for it.

- **The metrics system.** "Shows respect with coworkers" has carefully defined metrics that the employees must meet: for instance, they must spend thirty minutes of dedicated time speaking eye-to-eye and without devices. Or, they must avoid making negative statements about each other, and if they do, they must follow that negative statement with three positives. Whatever the metrics, the employees would have a scorecard that would objectively quantify their efforts.

Neither approach is perfect, but the latter gives you considerably more information to work from. After all, your employees could be making a good-faith effort and sincerely believe they're taking steps in the right direction when in reality they're continuing to fall into the same patterns. They're not trying to cheat the system, but they aren't able to be fully objective and may not know what they need to work on.

If you are not measuring it, you're not managing it. By clearly defining what information you need to see and making that information available to the right stakeholders, you remove the guesswork and create the means to move your business forward.

ANALYTICS IN ACTION

At the Bon-Ton stores, 240 merchants across sixty buying offices were having difficulty managing one million active products across 272 stores. Similar to the time and motion studies of yesteryear, it was uncovered that these 240 merchants were spending 40 percent of their workweek manually cobbling together data—valuable time that was intended to identify market opportunities. Delays from merchants manually evaluating $8 billion–$10 billion worth of purchases via binders of paper resulted in missed in-season buying opportunities.

By automating, the mundane, manual data work was reduced by 80 percent and they were able to better manage the business as was shown by a 10 percent reduction in markdown dollars with improved inventory allocation. Similarly, by utilizing live product images vs. the old text descriptions, merchants were able to instantly visualize MK logo bags performing better than even the vendor expected and recommended. This drove a quick response buy to capture the sales trend that had never been seen before.

In another case, SKU product reviews used to take 1.5 days, but with on-demand information at their fingertips, merchants could better manage the entire product portfolio (e.g., apparel color proliferation was analyzed and determined that the sales of fourteen colors in long dresses could analytically be captured with only eight of those colors). So, inventory dollars were moved resulting in an overall 20 percent reduction in SKU count.

Now that the data was cleaned and systematized, other unexpected benefits became apparent: vendors could perform their own reporting via a vendor portal and that reduction in workload allowed labor shifting so that new strategic initiatives could be tackled (e.g., close to home and market localization).

—Jimmy Mansker, former EVP, planning and allocation and replenishment, The Bon-Ton stores. Current head of agricultural solutions e-commerce and aftermarket solutions commercial solutions product management, CNH Industrial

PART 4

MONETIZING YOUR DATA

CHAPTER 10

WHO IS THIS INFORMATION FOR?

Have you ever wondered why phone numbers are broken up into sets of three digits, three digits, and then four digits? Or why zip codes are only five digits? Or why social security numbers are broken up into three-two-four number sets? The answer is that these presentations make the information easier to digest. The human brain may be capable of a lot, but it cannot handle too much information at once.

We, even when trying to be helpful, often overload people with too much information and let them sort out the details for themselves. However, when we do this, one of two things is bound to happen. The first is analysis paralysis. With so much information and so many different potential routes to take, we end up making no decision at all. For example, to select which flight to take from Dallas to Atlanta Monday morning, you are better off not seeing every scheduled route for your chosen airline for that day. If you do, you'll be flooded with so much information that you'll likely struggle to make sense of it all.

The second is a phenomenon called the paradox of choice; the more choices we have, the less likely we are to choose anything at all (which, as we discussed in chapter 2, is the worst decision you can make). When we *do* finally make a choice, we begin to fear whether we made the right one. After all, while we all accept that sometimes things don't play out like expected, we're far less willing to admit that sometimes *we* made the wrong decision.[9] So, we slip into CYA mode, readying ourselves to shift the blame or point the finger in a moment's notice.

Often, CYA mode compels us to recheck our work over and over again just so we can say "we looked it over ten times" in the event the insight doesn't play out favorably. While being thorough is certainly something to be admired, every time we recheck our work, we fall victim to the law of diminishing returns. We spend more time

---

9. In analytics, we're careful to distinguish between being wrong and being incorrect. When you're wrong, that means you did something you shouldn't have; when you're incorrect, you did the best with what you had but you weren't right. The best way to think about this is having a really good hand in poker doesn't always win and it would be wrong to bet against it. One that should win 80 percent of the time means it will also lose one out of five times.

and more money, but we see less and less benefit for our efforts in terms of ROI. The truth is, in most cases, looking something over and over again is not going to lead us to a better answer.

When it comes to preparing your information for your end users, it's important to avoid these two outcomes at all costs. It's better to give someone only the information absolutely necessary for them to understand a concept or complete a task. Depending on who that person is, this can look a lot of different ways. For instance, imagine that you're a department manager at an apparel store. You spend most of your time on the floor interacting with customers and staff. Since you don't have regular access to a laptop, your primary computer is a mobile device, either a tablet or a smartphone. The best way for you to receive important information, then, would be in a mobile-friendly format.

Alternatively, if you're a regional manager, someone who spends considerable time traveling between stores and departments, your needs are a little different. First, while you're still mobile, you probably carry a tablet or laptop with you. Second, because of the scope of your work, you need to work with a larger data set. The delivery team would still want to limit your information to only what's necessary for you to do your job, but that information would be more robust and be better suited for a tablet or laptop.

Whoever you're delivering information to, it's important that you understand who this person is, what information they need, and what the best means of delivery is. In this chapter, we'll discuss the different kinds of people using your information and then explore best practices for how to deliver them information in a way that's easy to digest and ready to drive action.

THE DIFFERENT TYPES OF INFORMATION USERS

Once you've collected your data, you have to think about the spectrum of users that will be utilizing it. There is a clear stratification of user types, so any one-size-fits-all approach will be DOA. Each type consumes information differently, so it's important that you consider not only the person's role in the company, but also how you should communicate with them to ensure they're getting the right information. When considering how to deliver your information to a given person, think about the user's technical capability, the sophistication of their analytics needs, their skills and familiarity with different tools, and the standardization and recurring nature of their information needs.

Speaking broadly, we've found that the different user types generally fall into one of the following three segments.

FIRST SEGMENT: KNOWLEDGE WORKERS

Knowledge workers make up the majority—typically 80 to 85 percent—of your information users and represent the typical kind of information usage. They will have guided access to information with dashboards that will help them understand the agreed-upon metrics most relevant to their jobs. They might sort, filter, and rank things to gain insights, but their information needs are fairly standard and predictable and focused on the daily needs in their normal course of business.

To get an idea of what your typical knowledge worker might look like, think back to the story of Janet from the book's introduction. Janet didn't need to work with any of the atomic-level data firsthand. She was working with information that was delivered to her in a guided-access format by way of an easy-to-use report that allowed her to digest the information, work with a local store manager to generate insights, and then take action.

Knowledge workers may not work directly with the granular data, but they're the most important conduit for driving ROI because they represent 80 to 85 percent of the information-using population. They don't need a great deal of technical competence or advanced tools—just basic computer knowledge and an understanding of web-based interfaces will do—but that in no way diminishes their value. The insights they produce with the information you deliver them directly lead to action, and therefore to your business's ability to monetize results. Delivering information to them in a guided environment may feel like you're limiting their access to your data (but you are only pointing them away from unneeded, distracting data), but by doing so you empower them to focus their efforts on the task at hand.

SECOND SEGMENT: SUPER USERS AND REPORT BUILDERS

This segment typically makes up about 10 to 15 percent of your users. While your knowledge workers simply use the information presented to them, super users and report builders will actually work with the more granular levels of data to build reports.

Here's where the super user sits in the process. First, the IT folks source the atomic-level data, transform it into basic information, and store it. Then, the super users access that basic information and use it to answer sporadic, next-level or nonstandard questions. Similarly, the report builders will help roll that basic info into higher-level summaries for rapid consumption by the knowledge workers.

Think of the super user or report builder's work as open ad hoc; they build one-off presentations that others may find useful for a specific purpose. As such, they have broader access to data that goes beyond the team's agreed-upon metrics. This puts them in a somewhat tricky situation. Both your super users and report builders work close enough with your data that they could mismatch some information or even crash the system with the wrong query.

The potential benefits that the super user brings, however, far outweigh the potential drawbacks. Because of their unique position and training, your super users are likely going to come up with multiple answers from differing angles to pressing business questions and help you get to the root of understanding your challenges and opportunities.

To get an idea of how a super user might interact with your information, think back to our online dating service example from chapter 8, where an error in data sorting led to an extreme overrepresentation of members in the area who were smokers. Using an advanced BI reporting and query tool, the super user would be the one to dive into the data and make sure it was being rolled up properly and in a way that represented the information accurately—in this case, creating a new attribute: "smoker friendly." While they're there, they might preempt any other problems by making sure that all user data could be sorted by different attributes, such as sexual orientation, marital status, hobbies, etc. Similarly, they might ask and seek answers to other questions that could potentially affect their user base, such as average income in a given area.

It's useful to think of your report builders as your delivery team. These are the people designated by the core team to work through the previously determined metrics, package them into useful information, and then disseminate those reports to the knowledge workers. So, while your super users are free to work through the data and find multiple approaches to the same basic question, they don't have free reign like the data scientists (see next section). They must work within the preset goals, value statements, and metrics as approved by the governance council.

THIRD SEGMENT: DATA SCIENTISTS

This segment is small and typically makes up only 2 to 3 percent of the users in your organization at most and are often limited to just a handful of people. Data scientists look at your data differently so that they can run important science projects. As data experts (they usually have a PhD or equivalent experience in statistics), your data scientist is able to create all kinds of crazy things that we mere mortals don't understand.

As the name implies, your data scientists focus on performing "science projects." Generally, the impetus for these projects comes from the data scientists themselves rather than from executive mandate (that's the super user's job). The data scientist, then, has great freedom to play with the data as they see fit as they search for unknown patterns and opportunities. As such, their research commonly requires data be assembled in unique, often messy, ways.

Using their own tools to grab never-before-seen data from anywhere they can, creating temporary tables as necessary, and building models to fill in missing data, data scientists utilize whatever data they deem relevant to generate new insights. It's important to note that, while both super users and data scientists are free to work with data in a variety of ways, they are generally not decision-makers, or anyone else whose actions actually capture ROI. Their job is to identify opportunities for the project owner (or executive sponsor) to act on, but they do not take action themselves.

DISSEMINATE THE INFORMATION AS THE USER WANTS TO RECEIVE IT

Again, your knowledge workers represent between 80 to 85 percent of the people who view your information—and they are the sole people to act on it. When thinking of your knowledge workers, it's important to note that a knowledge worker can occupy any level of the business. They can be a regional manager, like Janet, or they can be your CEO.

That said, there is a difference between how a regional manager needs to view and use information versus how your CEO does. To that end, your analytics system should be set up to disseminate information in a way that makes sense for each of them and empowers them to generate insights and take action.

Because your knowledge workers can occupy different levels or departments of your organization, you will have different kinds of knowledge workers. The highest-level executives, like the CEO, will have a high level of access to all kinds of metrics (generally via a KPI Management or Executive Dashboard) because that information is essential for them to make good decisions. Other knowledge workers, like someone in HR, for instance, would have access to information about the company's employees, while someone in another department would only have limited access to the employees under them.

The point of this is not to limit what others are able to see, but to empower them to generate insights and take action in the areas where they can be most effective. For instance, as the regional store manager, Janet needs to see different information than the department manager does. The department manager needs to be out on the floor interacting with customers, not creating insights on a strategic level. For the department manager, the information disseminated to them would be simple and action driven: "Here's the opportunity. Call these five customers and get on it."

Below the department manager, a salesperson would need even less information: "Here's the contest that's kicking off this week. Every time you sell product X, your name gets put into a drawing for a trip to the Caribbean." Or, every time a customer buys something, the salesperson gets a small reminder alert at the point-of-sale terminal to ask if that high-status customer wants free gift wrapping.

Each of these knowledge workers—the regional manager, the department manager, and the salesperson—are working off the same underlying data set. The difference is that, for each worker, that data has been rolled into easy-to-digest information specifically tailored to how they will consume and interact with it. They are interacting with the data in the manner that best fits their needs. Knowledge workers go right to a dashboard, while others may be given a powerful tool to access the data directly because they need that additional power. Whatever the specifics, the goal is to deliver only the most important information to the knowledge worker as quickly as possible so they can move from login to decision in the fewest clicks possible. Anything else adds costs, which then reduces ROI.

BE EFFECTIVE WITH THE LEAST INFORMATION POSSIBLE

One time, an analytics team that I was in charge of gave too much power to our knowledge workers (in this case, it was a campaign management specialist) giving them access to both the service and billing addresses of our customers.

This may not seem like a big deal, but businesses regularly have different service addresses than billing addresses. When the knowledge workers pulled the address list for a direct mail campaign, for whatever reason, they combined the billing addresses with the service address zip codes. As a result, many of our direct mail pieces were returned for having an undeliverable address. It wasn't the biggest analytics problem we could have had, but the mistake still cost us.

From that experience, we learned an important lesson: empower your team to be effective with the least information possible—and present your information with the right end user in mind.

The human brain is easily overloaded. The more information you give it, the more likely it is that it will make an error. By keeping things simple, user-friendly, and, above all, actionable, you dramatically increase your likelihood for success and reduce the chances of your end users making an innocent—but nevertheless costly—error. If you can do this, then the road to converting information into insight becomes a lot easier to travel.

ANALYTICS IN ACTION

Data benefits not-for-profits just as it does Fortune 1000 companies. St. David's Foundation in Austin invests over $75 million each year back into the local community in central Texas. The annual budgeting process used to require the CFO to meet individually with each cost center manager to walk through their budgets. At two to three hours per meeting and across upwards of twenty-five budget areas, this task took weeks, not just in sit-down meetings but also for each cost center manager to fill out their individual spreadsheets and for the CFO to then roll all of those spreadsheets into one common format and translate into one common language (e.g., HR might call a certain GL code something different than communications might call it.)

The answer was obvious: a simple analytic tool with data entered once. With a focus on clarity and ease of use for the cost center managers, the aggregated data would be combined, and the CFO would make all changes directly in the tool—forecasting, overriding actuals to planned numbers, etc.

Not only did this save each manager a full day of data entry and the interview process but gave back over two weeks to the CFO herself. Additionally, the CFO was able to share accurate and more timely approved budget numbers back down to each area along with the latest financials at everyone's fingertips. Previously there was no time for iterative budget reviews; now quarterly reviews are improving cost center alignment. But most importantly, there are benefits to the foundation.

By no longer getting bogged down with minutia, people could devote more energy to the mission itself and the more relevant problems with the community at large. And that freed-up energy has allowed investigations into ways to provide new community benefits.

—Blake Holman, former CIO, St. David's Foundation

CHAPTER 11

DELIVERING INSIGHTS

In chapter 2, we told the story of the energy retailer who thought they had two hundred thousand accounts, but in actuality only had thirty-five thousand. Central to this discovery was an account, specifically a Pizza Hut, that was sixty-three days past due. According to the energy retailer's practices, this kind of delinquency meant the account needed to be called and notified that their power would be cut off in ten days.

After further investigation, we came upon a startling discovery: the business owner who owned this Pizza Hut owned nine other Pizza Hut locations as well—and all of them got their electricity from our client. In isolation, the data showed an overdue bill at the Pizza Hut location, which was true (remember, data is always fact). But once we were able to roll together a better view of that data, we produced new information. There was a wealthy entrepreneur who owned ten Pizza Hut locations, but the energy retailer had been treating each separate location like it was a separate customer.

As we looked into the information further, we saw that nine of the ten Pizza Hut locations were current on their bills. It was only the one restaurant that was sixty-three days overdue. Otherwise, the customer's billing history across locations was exceptional. From this information, we were ready to begin generating insights.

The key insights fell to the sales consultant. After reviewing the information, they concluded that it didn't make any sense to call the customer and threaten to turn their power off if they didn't pay soon. Instead, they would take a gentler approach. First, they would check with the billing department and see if they had any issues on the billing side. Second, they would reach out to the owner, see if everything was okay, and ask if there was anything they could do to help or serve them better.

The sales consultant's insight was spot-on. After the billing department was alerted to the potential problem, they determined that they had some unknown internal billing system issue, and the bills for that location hadn't been sent out correctly. Soon, they had fixed the error, boosted customer satisfaction, avoided customer churn (remember, threatening the one late-paying location actually put ten locations at risk) and saved themselves the embarrassment of making a threatening call when they were the ones in error. Best of all, they were able to improve the cash flow problem generated by late bills, providing the necessary ROI for their efforts.

In this chapter, you're going to learn how to convert information into insights, just like our sales rep did. Here's where the art and science of analytics are in full force. Up to this point of the book, the analytics process has largely been driven by three factors: governance, process, and technology. However, because insights can't be repeated, documented, or understood, they belong in the capable hands of our human users.

DIFFERENT SEGMENTS SEEK DIFFERENT INSIGHTS

Depending on whether you're a knowledge worker, a super user, or a data scientist, you might be asking different questions, each with varying degrees of immediacy.

Analytics and Reporting: Differing Needs

TYPICAL USAGE		ADVANCED USAGE
INSIGHTS	**INVESTIGATIONS**	**SCIENCE PROJECTS**
↓	↓	↓
Daily type question in the normal course of business:	Investigations needed sporadically but not a pre-determined question to ask:	Special need what-if scenarios requiring data to be put together uniquely:
"e.g., How is product X selling versus the plan, and is there sufficient inventory on hand?"	*"e.g., Is product Y's poor performance that much out of line versus similar products last year?"*	*"Is weather or foot traffic driving more of the gains on Product Z's growth over the last 3 years?"*

Analytics and Reporting: Typical Information User Spectrum

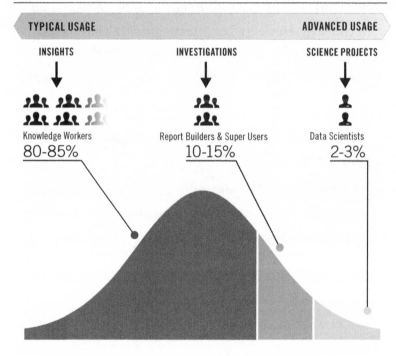

TYPICAL USAGE		ADVANCED USAGE
INSIGHTS	**INVESTIGATIONS**	**SCIENCE PROJECTS**
↓	↓	↓
Knowledge Workers	Report Builders & Super Users	Data Scientists
80-85%	10-15%	2-3%

Most numerous and most immediate is the knowledge worker, who needs questions answered such as: "How is product X selling versus the plan, and is there sufficient inventory on hand?" Having the answer to this question is needed in the normal daily course of business and produces the insights needed to capture all of the currently fastest-selling products (not the stars that are already known, but the ones that weren't as big as sellers last year and that are readily reorderable).

Next is the super user, who asks questions like: "Is product Y's poor performance that much out of line versus similar products last year?" While product Y is a new product, it's not selling as well as expected. But what's the reason? Is the product actually performing poorly, or did the company overplan and overestimate performance? To get to that information, the super user has to go to other source systems whose data hasn't been utilized before. It must be determined how that data can be merged with, and into, the standardized data in the reporting repository the knowledge worker utilizes (e.g., which items last year act as the best proxy for product Y this year?). An investigation yields the insight that, yes, they were a little overzealous and had overestimated performance. All told, product Y is not performing out of line from what similar products did last year.

Finally, there is the data scientist, who wonders: "Is

weather or foot traffic driving more of the gains on product Z's growth over the last three years?" After grabbing data from other source systems and merging them all together with some key data from outside the company, the data scientist performs numerous science experiments and determines that weather is indeed a major driver of this product. If the forecast is going to be wetter in the coming months, they will need to order more of product Z in order to capitalize on an opportunity.

As you can see from these examples, the different user segments seek answers to different types of questions. Because those questions differ so much between predictability, their repeatable nature, and the amount of time that can be spent and still capture value, the types of tools and the way the data integrates into the information user's workload and processes are key to successfully capturing positive ROI.

WHAT TO DELIVER

Now that you have an idea of the kinds of insights that can be delivered by the different types of end users at your company, it's time to set them up for success. The following recommendations build off our discussion in the previous chapter, mapping a specific set of dos and don'ts to empower your end users to take action and move the needle for your business.

IGNORE THE TAILS

Everybody already knows the very best-performing and the very low-performing products, sales regions, and employees. Because you already know it, you're not likely to change an action with more information about the same thing.

So, ignore it.

Remember, the tails on either end of your bell curve—the already-known stars and dogs—only represent about 5 to 10 percent of your total information on your products, sales regions, or employees. Also keep in mind that they represent the extreme ends of the spectrum and they are hard to do anything with, as there are no actions to take. For example, you already know the hottest-selling toy during Christmas season, but it's so hot that the vendor is out of inventory and is no longer taking reorders. Similarly, you know the biggest disappointment toy you stocked up on for Christmas, but it's such a dud that you've already marked it down twice. Besides, since it's not selling in any other stores, it doesn't make sense to take on the additional costs of transferring it. That information may have some value, but it is not representative of the other 90 to 95 percent of your information, which is where the true opportunities for insights lie.

In the old days, the general store owner understood this

quite well. He knew *everything*—not only how their stars and dogs were performing but also how everything else was performing. However, while this may have been easy to manage with a limited selection of items and a relatively small amount of customers and employees, it wasn't scalable.

Without analytics, the effort required to create that kind of intimacy would be prohibitively expensive to try—and nearly impossible to accomplish even if you did. With analytics, we can provide all the information across the entire portfolio to the knowledge worker. This is the information that can lead to surprising insights and drive action—not the tails on either end that have been studied ad nauseam.

Political campaigns understand this principle all too well. They know that they already have the vote on the extreme side of whatever side of the political spectrum they represent. However, those extremes only represent 10 to 15 percent of the voting population at most. Instead of focusing their advertising dollars on the extremes, they focus on how they can get the other 80 percent of voters to line up with their cause. Where should they spend their time? Where *shouldn't* they spend their time? By looking inside the bell curve rather than to the extremes, they are able to determine exactly where they should allocate their advertising dollars.

On the business side of things, imagine that you manufacture pipe fittings. One type of fitting has been selling like gangbusters; you can't even keep up with demand. However, you already know this fact and you've already maxed out your manufacturing capabilities, so there's nothing else you can do with this information. Similarly, certain other fittings aren't selling well at all, so you've dramatically reduced manufacturing of those products.

But what about the middle? By diving into that information, you may discover other products that need a manufacturing boost, and others that need a little less— both things that you can actionate on. In this case, the best way to monetize your data is to review and manage your entire portfolio of products so that you can maximize output for your whole business. Here, by "review and manage," we don't mean using a computer screen to manually review 100 percent of the items, as that would likely be time and cost prohibitive. Instead, a better approach would be to carefully define some guardrails, either by automated rules in the data or through notified alerts on only the exceptions you need to look at.

SELF-EXPLANATORY INFORMATION ONLY

There is no job description for knowledge workers that says, "Fool around with data and try to make things happen with it."

Instead, their job description is more like, "Build and manage relationships with vendors that supply products and services to maximize revenue." To help our knowledge workers live up to that job description, we need to empower them to move from information to insight as quickly as possible. This means the information needs to be self-explanatory—no need for a dictionary, no need for a phone call to coworkers who might know, nothing. They should be able to look at the information and instantly know what it means. That's information at your fingertips.

When crafting self-explanatory information, a few things to consider:

- **Don't give them too much.** Just like we talked about in the last chapter, if you overload them with information, they're not going to see the most valuable pieces.
- **Be clear.** Vague information means they will have to spend time trying to figure out the differences and overthinking it. That's cost.
- **Make it trustworthy.** If the numbers don't add up or if something doesn't appear right, they're going to spend five to ten times the time they should be spending to get their insights. That's a waste of time.

Think of self-explanatory information the way you think about the dashboard on your car. None of the readings—speedometer, odometer, fuel gauge, or check engine light—leave any room for interpretation. You know exactly what they're trying to tell you at only a moment's glance.

UTILIZE CLEAR AND CONSISTENT TIME-SLICED INTERVALS

Most of the information knowledge workers will be using is time-sliced in increments that are daily, weekly, monthly, and upward. This is necessary if you want to change the behavior of not only the knowledge worker but also of the whole company. After all, you don't want to change the way a single employee spends their marketing dollars or approaches the recruiting process. You want to change how *everyone* does it.

There are a couple basic reasons why analytics works best with time-sliced data. First, they're easy to understand. They have a clear beginning and end period, and therefore they're easy to compare against other periods—yesterday, last week, last quarter, this time last year, etc.

Second, the facts are the same no matter who looks them up. If one worker claims that bills for pipe fittings were 10 percent less than they were the previous summer, that's a fact. Anyone else who's interested is free to rerun the report and verify that worker's claim.

Real-time information is a little trickier since it's changing all the time. If I asked you how many planes have taken off today, that number will be different by the time you finish reading this paragraph than it was when I first asked it. When information is changing so rapidly, it's hard to get everyone on the same page.

Other times, real-time information simply isn't needed. If you're a supply chain VP, for instance, you want to know how many packages move through your warehouse every day, every week, every year, etc. However, you probably don't need to know that today, by about 3:00 p.m., 38,562 packages had moved through the facility. That's incomplete and changing information and better suited to the warehouse manager who is in charge of the tactical operations. To drive your decision-making, you need complete information that's unambiguous and doesn't change.

That said, when real-time changes in action are occurring, then real-time information is the only way to go. For instance, imagine you work at a nuclear power plant. If at any point the reading on a certain dial exceeds a certain level, you immediately want to shut down the system. In that case, that real-time information is important to know. It's a simple, quick strike that allows you to keep your finger on the pulse of what's going on but that otherwise doesn't drive decision-making.

As this example shows, real-time information is great for supporting real-time action changes. However, that's only relevant to workers who have jobs with real-time and on-demand responsibilities—in other words, people who can't randomly leave their post to grab a cup of coffee without formally putting someone else in charge. These real-time-bound workers are not the same as the knowledge workers and other information users who are going to help you monetize your data.

KEEP FINANCIAL REPORTING SEPARATE FROM THE OTHER REPORTS

Financial data is different from other kinds of data. Accountants at heart, your financial team needs their numbers to be accurate down to the penny. Knowledge workers, because they're only looking for direction, need their numbers to be accurate, but not exact. In other words, direction matters, but precision does not.

Financial reporting also brings a lot of jargon with it that isn't used anywhere else in your business, such as allocating overhead and recognizing revenue. Those are important measures for the financial team, but they are not the kinds of measures that change a business. Additionally, they are not facts, but rather invented ways of distributing things that can't be done in the natural flow of business.

ANALYTICS IN ACTION

Four years ago, Southwest Airlines had a deeply experienced team of subject matter experts (SMEs) sitting in a command center manually determining the adjustments to make to a complicated flight schedule based on weather disruptions and other unusual situations. But with an expanding aircraft fleet, new routes (including international destinations), growing passenger volumes, and additional service to airports known for heavy traffic and congestion (e.g., LaGuardia), a more automated approach was required.

How to do that? The first challenge was sourcing massive amounts of data in real time: five hundred thousand daily passengers (head counts; understanding of "whole journey," not just the segment; priority flyers); twenty-three thousand crew members (fluid schedules due to flexible union contracts; FAA legalities); 750 aircraft (aircraft configuration; real-time location; pending maintenance needs); and four thousand flights to one hundred airports daily (departure/arrival stations; available seats; flight path). Then algorithms were deployed: what if there's a delay from fog in San Francisco, or a pilot becomes ill before a Chicago connecting flight, or tarmac delays in Atlanta put the crew members out of compliance, or the current aircraft needs to finish the day in Phoenix to undergo maintenance that is only performed at that hangar?

The solution was a data-driven optimization engine that provides flight guidance for the entire network at a push of a button. For instance, "Chicago will be shut down for four hours due to a snowstorm—give me three scenarios for getting our customers where they need to go with the least amount of delays despite the storm." This rich information, combined with the art and expertise of the SMEs themselves, has resulted in a significant improvement in on-time performance during days with irregular operations—which is basically every day for an airline as large as Southwest Airlines. Each day, that translates directly into tens of thousands of passengers being on time or less delayed, which in turn means happier customers, avoidance of delay disruptions and the accommodations and overtime costs associated with them, as well as improved compliance in a safety-first environment.

—Jennifer Paine, senior director, technology, Southwest Airlines

To give an example, imagine that you work for an auto manufacturer. You estimate that you will sell X number of cars in the subcompact group next year, so you allocate $1,000 of headquarters cost to that car. Suddenly, you discover that you're on track to sell three times as many of those cars as you expected. This means that your overhead cost for manufacturing those subcompacts is three times as much as well. That cost matters to your financial team, but it doesn't matter to the rest of the business, which is only focused on the product, whether it's being manufactured at a rate to match demand, and whether it's being sold. Because these numbers aren't relevant to any metrics focused on decision-making, they should be kept separate from the rest of the information for nonfinance knowledge workers.

This isn't to say that you shouldn't have financial reporting—you absolutely should; just know that it's different from your operational reporting and therefore should be treated differently. Even when you incorporate sales reporting into your analytics, the reports should be different for the sales team than for the financial team. At Armeta Analytics, we even make sure to color code the reports differently just so there is no ambiguity between the different types of reports.

In that way, it's not much different than what we discussed in the previous chapter; different end users have different needs. Just like you wouldn't deliver the same information to the CEO as you would to a regional manager, you wouldn't deliver the same information to your sales team as you would to your financial team.

GETTING INFORMATION TO THE DECISION MAKERS

If it took you a full two minutes to look up a song every time you heard something you liked on the radio, you'd never do it; it's too much effort for too little reward. However, if you could just tap the screen on your smartphone and get the answer instantly, you'd use a tool like that all the time (maybe even to your detriment).

Whether in music or in business (or even the music business), no one wants to spend much time to get their information. They want it in the most consumable fashion possible, and they want it in the moment. A key goal of a good analytics program, then, is to deliver the least amount of information to your decision-makers in the most accessible way possible so that they can begin generating valuable insights.

In other words, you don't want to data dump. It may seem like a good idea to give your decision-makers as much information as possible, so they have a "complete" picture, but in reality all you're doing is obscuring the most important information.

Unless you're a lawyer—in which case it's considered a best practice to overload your opposition with so much information that they can't find the proverbial smoking gun—give your decision-makers and knowledge workers a break. Only give them what's essential to do their jobs. If they need more information, they'll ask.

Make no mistake, this is going to take work. It often takes more time to be concise and on target. As the old joke goes, "I was going to write you a short letter, but I didn't have the time, so I wrote you a long one instead." In this case, the time investment is absolutely worth it—and as long as you're not spending 80 percent of your time collecting and sorting data, you'll have the time to spare here.

HOW TO DELIVER YOUR INFORMATION

Your reporting package must be action oriented, so it changes behavior and creates ROI. To deliver an action-oriented reporting package, use the following approaches.

HAVE A CLEAR LEXICON AND UNAMBIGUOUS LABELS

Again, your knowledge workers shouldn't be spending

any time looking at information to figure out what it means. In other words, you never want to hear, "Well, it says sales. Is that gross sales or net sales? Does that include coupons? What about returns?"

Remember the fuel pump story from chapter 4, where we explored all the different terms and considerations different team members might use to define a pump? This is where taking the time to establish a clear, unambiguous lexicon pays off. The clearer you were up front, the less trouble you'll have here on the back end. For instance, if "sales" doesn't paint a clear picture, get more specific and say, "Net sales adjusted for returns."

SCREENS MUST ALWAYS DISPLAY EXACT DETAILS

Inevitably, people are going to photocopy, screenshot, or otherwise capture the report you sent them and store in another (incomplete) form. Because of this, you want whatever information that person might have captured to stand on its own. To remove any ambiguity, consider the following questions:

- When was the report created?
- What is the age of the data?
- Are the labels unambiguous?
- What time frame is being presented?
- What region does this report pertain to?

You can't stop your knowledge workers from capturing or copying your reports (and you want that information being distributed far and wide), so empower them to have as complete a picture as possible so that when they show a pie chart to another coworker and say, "Sales are down 20 percent," that coworker won't greet them with a blank stare.

ALL TOTALS SHOULD MATCH AND ADD UP TO 100 PERCENT

It's easy to manipulate numbers in a way that's misleading or that negatively impacts decision-making. For instance, think of the companies interested in selling gambling advice for sports betting. They'll take a mailing list of ten thousand names and message that group in the days or weeks leading up to a game. Six thousand people will receive predicted victories related to one team (the favorite), while the remaining four thousand people will receive predicted victories related to the other team (the underdog). No matter the outcome, they will be right in the eyes of one segment or the other.

The next week, they repeat the process with the winning segment. Then they do it again the week after. By this point, a narrow subsection of those initial ten thousand people has only seen this company predict winner after winner, including the underdog in the appropriate week.

They don't know that the company has been hedging their bets by sending different messages to different groups. From their perspective, that company only picks winners.

If they had all the information—who else the company talked to and whether they shared the same information with everyone—these people might think differently about what this company was up to. But they don't. And because of that, they are unable to see the truth. When the numbers don't add up to 100 percent, you can tell any story you want.

Say the information you're delivering includes a histogram with sectors broken into 32 percent, 25 percent, and 41 percent. It may look good, but the totals only add up to 98 percent. As soon as your knowledge worker notices this discrepancy, two big problems are likely to occur:

1. Your knowledge worker won't trust the data because they'll know it's not the complete picture, and therefore they won't make a decision to move your business forward.
2. There's something wrong with your data that has gone unnoticed until right now.

There could be any number of reasons why your percentages don't total up to 100. For instance, a sales rep could have accidentally forgotten to categorize a closed sale.

Or, an employee wasn't assigned to their proper department in the system, and, therefore, their sales didn't get captured in the departmental sales query.

In all our years in the analytics business, we've yet to encounter a sizeable data set that is entirely error-free. For instance, we've seen companies run a sales analysis by state, only to find that the total sales in that analysis didn't match up with the total number of sales they knew they had. So, what went wrong? They hadn't accounted for sales in Washington, DC, which isn't a state, but still had to be accounted for in the report. How do you handle territories like Puerto Rico and Guam? Do you want to include overseas military bases or not?

Your last line of defense for catching errors like these is to make sure the numbers always add up to 100 percent. Put anything unexpected or unusual in an "other" bucket. If you don't, you can be sure that some important data is unknowingly being excluded.

USE VISUALS TO ACCELERATE CONSUMPTION

As the saying goes, a picture is worth a thousand words. Whether as a chart, a graph, colorized text, or even a relevant photograph, visuals help your knowledge workers consume information as fast as possible.

For instance, say you're trying to convince your knowledge workers that your competitors are doing a better job with their displays in the premium denim section. You could write up a few paragraphs to illustrate your point, or you could just include two pictures—one of your competitor's display, and one of yours—to make the same point. In fact, in cases like these, the images will likely make the point *better* than any write-up ever could.

Visuals are so effective that we've seen clients take the same approach with their vendors that they take with their knowledge workers. Instead of arguing over what a product is called or what color it is, they just insert a photograph of the item in question, and everyone is immediately on the same page.

For this reason, we don't consider visuals just a good idea, but a necessity. If your reports are chock full of rows and columns of data and nothing else, then you're probably not on the right path with your efforts.

IT'S ALL ABOUT THE DECISION

Time is money. As quickly as possible, your knowledge workers need to consume the information and develop an insight. Until that actionable decision is made, and the behavior is changed, there is no ROI. It's all expense.

For instance, say that your team decides to train all the front desk people at your hotel to offer a suite upgrade for $29. Training costs money. It costs money to design the program. It costs money to write, format, and print the supporting materials. It costs money to send people to the training and conduct it. Every step of the way, it's expense, expense, expense until the first time a member of your front desk team says to a guest, "Would you like to upgrade to a suite for $29?"

Once that decision occurs, then you begin to capture your ROI.

The same principle applies to your knowledge workers. It costs money to source data, roll it up to useful information, present it to them, and empower them to generate their insights. Until that person or the people they're in charge of change their behaviors, then it's all expense with no ROI. However, as we'll see in our final chapter, if you can change that behavior, then the ROI can come in many ways.

CHAPTER 12

TAKING ACTION

Now that you've completed this prescriptive process for guaranteed analytics, it's important that we take a chapter to put all the pieces together.

Throughout the book, we've shared examples of the challenges many companies experienced along the way to analytics adoption and what they did to address them. Many of those companies were able to grow beyond their early struggles and monetize their business through analytics. In this chapter, we'll share some of those stories to give you a few examples of analytics done right. While we've fictionalized the brand names out of respect to our clients (we would never divulge our clients' proprietary information), the stories themselves are all real.

THE SPORTING GOODS RETAILER

When we first started working with Game On, a large sporting goods retailer, they had already figured out the logistics of how to put product in their stores and which products to pick. They had their merchandising down, but they were interested in finding other ways to increase their revenue without adding much in additional costs.

Our analysis revealed an opportunity around market basket analysis. We wanted to improve how they analyzed product mix by transactions over time, enable better merchandising and marketing decisions off of that knowledge, and drive up the average market basket size.

In other words, our goal was to add just one item for every twenty to thirty transactions that occur. If we could do that, we believed we would see an increase in sales by 2 to 4 percent across the company.

On the analytics side, we had to understand the data by market basket over time. The BI team discovered that Game On could be smarter on the upsale. For instance, customers who bought baseball gear usually bought a Gatorade. Throughout the store, we were able to identify similar opportunities, highlighting the exact products that should be recommended for upsale in combination with other items.

With this information, the merchandising team sprang into action and began displaying related market basket items together on the shelf—including Gatorade by the baseball section. At the same time, the marketing team began working on more relevant promotions in order to raise customer awareness of related products. Even the website team got in the game and began finding clever ways to offer relevant upsales.

In the end, by being smarter about how they merchandised in stores, how they promoted at checkout, and how they marketed to customers, Game On was able to persuade customers to add additional items to their basket. This resulted in tens of millions of dollars a year in increased sales.

THE MULTILOCATION DISCOUNT CHAIN

Like Game On, Discount All was looking for ways to encourage customers to buy more items. They were sourcing plenty of data from their point-of-sale systems, but they hadn't been able to turn that data into useful, actionable information.

After working through their data, we identified an opportunity around product affinity. Our goal was to determine the top one hundred items sold over the previous twelve months, determine what items usually sold with those products, and incentivize customers who weren't making those purchases together to begin making those affinity product purchases.

To put this in more practical terms, imagine that one of the most-purchased items was a can of pork and beans. We set out to identify the five items that were purchased most frequently along with those cans of pork and beans—such as hot dogs, hot dog buns, barbecue sauce, potato chips, and macaroni and cheese.

In an example of the science of analytics meeting the art, we also had to work to sort out some noise in the channel. Our initial reporting produced redundant information. For instance, our data showed that the most frequently purchased items alongside cans of pork and beans were other cans of pork and beans in different sizes. The data also separated out and categorized the many different kinds of macaroni and cheese and chips.

From a computer's standpoint, these may have been different items. But from a practical standpoint, we were only interested in the broad categories: beans, macaroni and cheese, and chips. In our next iteration, we were able to show only correlated products that were different from the "pork and beans" merchandising class.

With that information, we then worked to identify all the

stores that were underperforming relative to the average. In other words, stores where customers still purchased cans of pork and beans but purchased the other five items at a lower rate. After determining who these underperformers were, we then worked with their knowledge workers to make them aware of the sales opportunity and how they might be able to capitalize on it. These opportunities included:

- Building awareness among store managers
- Using different signage in the store
- Changing the merchandising of items to be nearer each other
- Placing ads for key and proxy items together in the local paper circular that showed the items together

The opportunity we identified only amounted to roughly $1,000 in additional weekly revenue per location per week. However, because Discount All had more than ten thousand locations, a $1,000 increase per store added up to $10 million in additional revenue per week. All we had to do was bring the underperforming stores closer to average, and we would easily reach that goal.

THE LIFESTYLE PRODUCT MANUFACTURER

Cold Container didn't have insight into how their products were selling across different distribution channels.

They were sourcing a good amount of data through their ERP system, but they weren't able to work with that data in a way that would help them make actual decisions. They were certain they were leaving money on the table, but unsure of where or how, they just kept up with the status quo, manufacturing and distributing their products without knowing how to make better investments or how to better manage their product offerings.

Their CEO badly wanted insights so she could get a better understanding of what their sales were like the previous day, week, and month. The Cold Container team had this data, and while the problem seemed simple enough, they spent months trying to develop a reliable way to access and synthesize it into useful information. Frustrated and confused, they eventually turned to us.

After spending some time with Cold Container to understand their needs and their challenges, we were finally able to tap into their underlying system, pull out data from nine thousand different tables, organize it in a way that made sense, and clearly define terms—such as the difference between an order, a shipment, and a sale. This enabled the Cold Container team to begin to see what they had been looking for and find new opportunities for their products.

We then began distributing the information we had organized to their inventory team, who were able to generate a variety of crucial insights. For instance, they realized they could double down on certain SKUs that were performing well and heavily reduce their SKU counts elsewhere. The result was fewer products and more investments in the products with the most upside, leading to a sales increase of over $3 million. This insight—sell more by carrying less—was risky, but it worked.

As we said in chapter 9, you can't manage what you can't measure. Before implementing their analytics program, Cold Container didn't even know how certain colors were performing relative to others. Blue, cerulean blue, light blue, and sky blue were all rolled up into the broad category of "blue," allowing a comparison to other color groups and providing trend insights. Once we were able to unlock their data and synthesize it into useful information, they were able to produce insights that transformed their understanding of their own product offerings.

WORK HARD NOW TO HAVE A DIFFERENTIATED COMPETITIVE ADVANTAGE LATER

We know analytics works. We know that people are taking money off the table with it. We know it's hard to do because the majority of people who attempt it aren't able to accomplish it. By doing this properly, you are able to create a unique competitive advantage in your business because you will be in the 20 percent that succeeds. You will sit confidently knowing that four out of five of your competitors cannot accomplish what you are doing.

Granted, this is easier said than done. Most of us are accustomed to acting tactically, to fighting fires, to addressing our immediate needs rather than our future needs. By its nature, thinking strategically is an abstract exercise, and our brains are hardwired to focus on the issues that are nearer and more urgent. The data may tell us what's going to happen next November and December, but if it's the middle of January and we're feeling burnt out, we may not be inclined to listen.

This is why the companies that come to us are almost always either thriving or dying. They're so overwhelmed with their day-to-day that they've completely lost a sense of the big picture and need a third party to help them break the cycle of firefighting and begin to think more strategically. It's not easy, but the companies that are able to commit and follow a prescriptive program for analytics inevitably see stunning results in the long run, leaving many to wonder why they hadn't done something like this sooner.

The difference between the companies that see these results and the companies that don't can be summed up in one word: action.

Thinking about your information is nice. If that's what you enjoy, then looking at a bunch of reports can be great entertainment. But, in reality, it's often no different than scrolling through news headlines or checking social media posts. However, no matter how much data you've collected, no matter how well you've looked at it, and no matter how readily available or consumable you've made it to your employees, if an insight isn't made and action isn't being taken, it's all for naught. With the guaranteed analytics process, the opportunity to take your business to the next level is staring you in the face. Now, it's up to you to take it.

CONCLUSION

YOUR JOURNEY TO GUARANTEED
ANALYTICS STARTS NOW

I met a guy named Kevin at a conference in Las Vegas. He'd been asked to head up an analytics effort for a large industrial products manufacturer. He was a hardworking, smart guy. His heart was in the right place, and he was excited about bringing analytics to his business.

During our conversation, Kevin was bragging to me about how he was buying all these different tools and sourcing so much data that it would "make my head spin"—and in so doing, improve the analytics capabilities of his company.

Kevin's intentions were great. He wanted to do the right thing, but his focus was in the wrong place.

Kevin failed.

Kevin was in the 80 percent group that finds analytics success elusive. Selecting useful tools is important. Adopting tools for the sake of it is not. Similarly, sourcing data is essential to a thriving analytics program. Sourcing data with no clear goals in mind, however, is an exercise in futility. Kevin had the right idea, but his efforts weren't tied to an actual decision or value statement.

Seven months into his effort, a lot of costs had been incurred, no specific value that got senior management's attention had been acquired, and they terminated the project. Kevin was surprised. I, while saddened, was not surprised in the least.

This is the reality for the majority of businesses who attempt to build an analytics program for their companies.

But this *isn't* going to be the reality for you and your business.

You are going to buck the trend and be one of the 20 percent of businesses whose analytics program succeeds.

Why? Because you know there's money being left on the table. You know the challenges that lie ahead of you, but you also know how to rise to meet them. You are the hero of this analytics journey—your team is behind you, your quiver is full, and now you're ready to go and get that pot of gold.

The question now is, what next?

DETERMINE WHERE YOU STAND

Now that you've read our prescriptive approach to guaranteed analytics, it's time to give yourself a self-diagnostic. Take a moment to consider your answers to the following questions:

- Do you have a clear P&L responsible exec owning and driving your analytics efforts?
- Do you have someone dedicated to lead the organizational makeup of your analytics team?
- Do you have a clear governance structure?
- Do you have a dedicated group of people who has worked on analytics projects before?
- Have you jointly documented the data-driven decision-making process?
- Do you have a clearly defined lexicon that everybody on your team has adopted?
- Is the term *analytics* understood in usage?
- Do you have clearly defined goals as values?
- What behavior change do you hope to bring about?
- Do you use your goals and values to drive tool adop-

tion and data sourcing, or do you want to just go get the data first?

- Is your program iterative, built around the idea of regular implementations on a frequent basis?
- Does information drive your business decisions?

Tally up your answers. If you answered "yes" to at least nine of these questions, then you're well on your way to analytics success. However, if you answered "no" to four or more, then your analytics program may be over before it begins.

If you fall into the latter camp, don't worry; even for the most well-intentioned, analytics success can be elusive. However, it's not too late. You can guarantee success by getting your team on the same page, working to deliver against a defined value proposition, and following the prescriptive process outlined in this book. After all, if you don't want to end up like the countless other businesses that fail to implement their analytics program, then you're going to have to do things differently.

We can think of plenty of companies out there who can confidently tick off every single item in this list. These are the Frito-Lays, FedExes, and Amazons of the world who are thriving because of their analytical ability. However, if you aren't from a company like that and if this doesn't sound like your organization, then you're likely going to need some hand-holding.

If that's the case, or if you simply don't have the capacity to drive your own analytics efforts internally, then a third-party analytics provider may be right for you, somebody who has been through this process dozens of times before and can steer you clear of the most common analytics mistakes.

That's where we come in. Armeta Analytics lives guaranteed analytics—we literally guarantee all of our work. We will hold your hand throughout the process and ensure you are in the minority 20 percent that succeed at analytics. You can solve even your most complex challenges with Armeta Analytics—a proven team of data scientists, engineers, and business executives whose sole focus is to find opportunities buried in your data. Leverage our decades of experience taking data in any format from any system and enabling our Fortune 1000 clients with the analytics they need to drive revenue, maximize profitability, and capture new customers.

We are so confident we can help you succeed that if we don't accomplish what we set out to accomplish, then you don't pay. *That's* guaranteed analytics.

ANSWER THE BELL

As we've said throughout this book, when it comes to building a successful analytics program, the odds are against you. Four out of five businesses that attempt analytics fail. There's no sugarcoating it: analytics is hard work.

But it's also not impossible. In fact, despite the challenges analytics poses, it's not the process itself that causes businesses to stumble. It's finding a prescriptive model that works, getting the key players on the same page, and sticking with the game plan.

You can be the one in five that makes it. All you have to do is take the blueprint for success outlined in this book, work with your team to implement it, and *stick with it*.

Many are called, but few are chosen. Now, it's up to you. When it's your turn to answer the bell, will you rise to the challenge?

ACKNOWLEDGMENTS

A special thanks to my parents, who have always worked so hard and made the necessary sacrifices in their lives so that I could even attend college and thus be put into a position to publish this book. There's no way to repay that kind of devotion, and I'm grateful for all they've given me.

I can never provide enough thanks to ever be even with my sister, Patty, for her always-present and effervescent excitement, combined with her universal and unconditional support in all I do.

Additionally, a special thanks to those who helped bring this book to life: To Ted Ingram for his punctilious help with selecting the words here to reflect what we do on our analytics projects on a day-in, day-out basis. And to Mark Platt and Kendall Creative for their assistance with the graphics that help make the book an easier read.

And to each of the execs who have shared such great stories from their actual careers for you, the reader, to be able to learn from them. Their stories really help bring this book to life. I am so pleased with their support and contributions. And it's an impressive list. Alphabetically:

- Bobby Aflatooni, SVP, infrastructure, **Howard Hughes Corporation**
- Todd Crosslin, VP, healthcare strategy, **Snowflake Computing**
- Brendan Hoffman, CEO, **Vince**
- Blake Holman, former CIO, **St. David's Foundation**
- Jimmy Mansker, head of agricultural solutions e-commerce and aftermarket solutions commercial solutions product management, **CNH Industrial**
- Robert Motion, director, workforce planning and strategy, intelligence, information and services, **Raytheon Company**
- Dan Murphy, regional director of sales (TOLA & LATAM), **Snowflake Computing**
- Jennifer Paine, senior director, technology, **Southwest Airlines**
- Ryan Seiders, cofounder, **YETI Coolers**
- Jim Stewart, **PhD in management science**
- Sam Wagar, VP, information technology, **Golub Corporation/Price Chopper Supermarkets**

ABOUT THE AUTHOR

JIM RUSHTON began his career in analytics working with some of the biggest consulting companies in the world, including Accenture, Deloitte Consulting, and IBM Global Services. Jim then moved to an executive position with Verizon, where he oversaw the company's customer and marketing information. Leveraging his experience across corporate America, he helped found Armeta Analytics. Since then, his team has helped dozens of Fortune 1000 companies learn how to look beyond the obvious and monetize their data. In his spare time, Jim likes to escape the urban landscape and spend time outdoors, chainsawing cedars, collecting rocks for a hand-built stone chapel, eating Texas's famous smoked brisket, and watching the sunset.

Made in the USA
Monee, IL
17 August 2021

75913987R00152